SEARCH

The Christian Experience

Iain A. S. Gray
Donald M. McFarlan

Blackie

$\boxed{S}\boxed{E}\boxed{A}\boxed{R}\boxed{C}\boxed{H}$

The Christian Experience

Blackie & Son Ltd
Bishopbriggs · Glasgow G64 2NZ
7 Leicester Place · London WC2H 7BP

First published 1984
Second Edition 1989

British Library Cataloguing in Publication Data

Gray, Iain A.S.
    Search. – (2nd ed.)
I. Title I McFarlan, Donald M. (Donald Maitland)
248.4

ISBN 0-216-92664-5   E.Pbk.
ISBN 0-216-92799-4   Pbk.

Photosetting and origination by Presentia Art, Horsham
Printed in Great Britain by Thomson Litho Ltd, Scotland

CONTENTS

THE SEARCH

Questions, Questions . . .

Look at the picture which is on the front and back covers of this book. It is a painting by the French artist Paul Gauguin which he painted on the island of Tahiti. Gauguin worked at it for a whole month at a time when he was suffering from great misery of body and mind. He gave the picture the strange title: *Where do we come from? What are we? Where are we going?* He said that it spoke to him of 'a fathomless enigma', that is, a riddle or puzzle that will always tease the mind.

- Gauguin traces the life cycle of man from the baby on the extreme right of the picture to the old woman in the extreme left. How many people are there in the picture?
- What do you think each of them is doing?
- Why do you think the old woman is covering her ears? (Note the various figures near her.)
- Why do you think she is painted in a crouching position?
- Which Jewish story with meaning lies behind the painting? (Note the fruit being plucked from the tree.)

Gauguin's picture asks questions which have always been in the mind of man. It is part of our nature to ask questions. In fact, this is one way of saying that man is different from other animals: he alone asks questions. Think of the endless questions a young child asks: 'Why is the sky blue?' 'Who made the trees?' 'Where did I come from?', and so on and on and on. And think of the countless questions you have to try to answer in every class in eleven years at school!

Some questions have definite answers and we learn them off by heart. Two and two make four, whether we like it or not, and common salt has the chemical formula NaCl. But our search for answers does not end with the definitions given in the dictionary or encyclopedia. What about these questions, for example:

- How did life begin?
- What is the relationship between man and other animals?
- Are there other forms of intelligent life in the universe?
- Am I here for a purpose, or is life meaningless?
- How free are we to make our own decisions?
- What happens after death?
- Is there a God, and if so, how does this affect us?

Jot down your initial comments on these questions. Some of the questions particularly in the earlier parts of the book are in the form of 'starter' questions, to encourage you to explore various ideas. As you read further in the book you will come across some of these questions again and you can explore them in the light of your further studies. It may be interesting to compare your first and later comments on these issues.

Questions such as these have teased and fascinated men and women all through the ages. Some of them in modern times can be answered by the sciences. One of the basic skills in the search for answers is to be able to recognize which field of study to turn to for help with a given answer. Is the answer to be found in astronomy, biology, psychology? Or is none of these appropriate or adequate?

Some questions have always been the proper concern of religion, and the various religious traditions of the world offer insight into them. Many of these questions are covered by the questions which Paul Gauguin posed with his picture:

Where do we come from?

What are we?

Where are we going?

We may wish to add one other question:

How do we get there?

Gauguin's three questions will for ever trouble the human mind. Our fourth question: How do we get there? comes from day-to-day living.

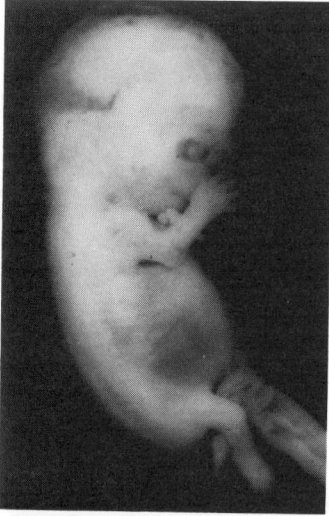

Where do we come from?

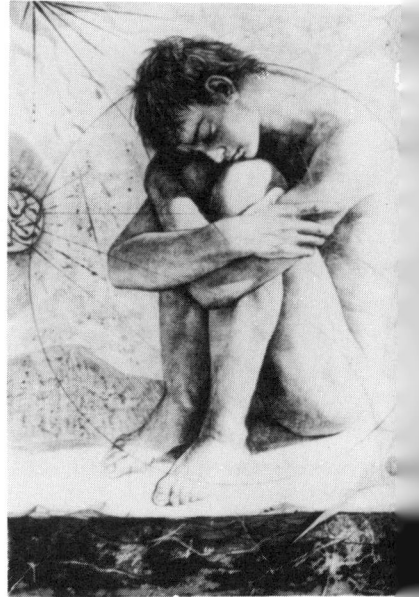

What are we?

Where are we going?

The Christian Experience

This book explores the Christian way of coming to terms with these questions. How do we find out what the Christian faith has to say? One obvious way would be to examine the beliefs which all the main branches of the Christian Church hold in common. For example, one very ancient basic statement of the Christian faith is *The Nicene Creed* which is still recited by Christian people all over the world:

'I believe in one God the Father Almighty, Maker of heaven and earth, and of all things visible and invisible:

And in one Lord Jesus Christ, the only-begotten Son of God, begotten of His Father before all worlds, God of God, Light of Light, Very God of Very God, begotten, not made, Being of one substance with the Father, by whom all things were made: who for us men, and for our salvation, came down from heaven, and was incarnate by the Holy Ghost of the Virgin Mary, and was made man, and was crucified also for us under Pontius Pilate. He suffered and was buried, and the third day He rose again according to the Scriptures, and ascended into heaven, and sitteth on the right hand of the Father. And He shall come again with glory to judge both the quick and the dead: whose kingdom shall have no end.

And I believe in the Holy Ghost, The Lord and Giver of Life, who proceedeth from the Father and the Son, who with the Father and the Son together is worshipped and glorified, who spake by the prophets. I acknowledge one Baptism for the remission of sins. And I look for the Resurrection of the dead, And the life of the world to come. AMEN.'

We shall hear about the Nicene Creed again when we look at the traditions of some of the main Churches of Christendom. But how does this ancient and confusing language help us with our four questions?

Where do we come from?

What are we?

Where are we going?

How do we get there?

Most of the language of the Nicene Creed seems unreal and far away from our search for meaning. The words and ideas do not belong to our 20th century, and they do not make sense of our life style.

Search

In our search we begin with people, not beliefs. To find out who the Christians are we look at the different *churches* in our community, because Christians live and worship not just as individuals, but as members of a Church.

We then turn to how Christians *worship*, weekly on a Sunday in their special places of worship, and daily in their own homes. For Christians, worship is rooted in the Church and in the *Bible*. The key to understanding the words and actions which take place during worship lies in the Bible. So we will explore some of the central passages of the Bible in our search for the Christian's answers to our questions.

The close link between the Bible and worship is clearly seen in the *festivals* of the Christian Church, where many of the customs are rooted in Bible stories. We will explore the two main festivals celebrated by Christians.

But just as the Church community has special times set aside in its life, so each individual Christian has his own special festivals or *personal milestones.* Worship and the Bible play a central part in the celebration of these important events.

The Bible, however, not only guides Christians in their worship and their community and personal celebrations. It also guides Christians in their *relationships* towards others – at home, in the local community, and at a national and international level. We will therefore examine what the Bible has to say about how Christians should live their daily lives.

But we have to keep in mind all the time that we live in the 20th century, and that the modern world has problems and practices unknown to the early days of the Christian tradition. How do the Churches and individual Christians apply the teaching of the Bible and their experiences of worship to the big *issues* of the 20th century?

Finally, we come back to our four questions:

Where do we come from?

What are we?

Where are we going?

How do we get there?

The Bible in worship
The Book of Gospels carried aloft during
an Orthodox service of worship

A festival
Re-enacting the Passion of Christ in Mexico

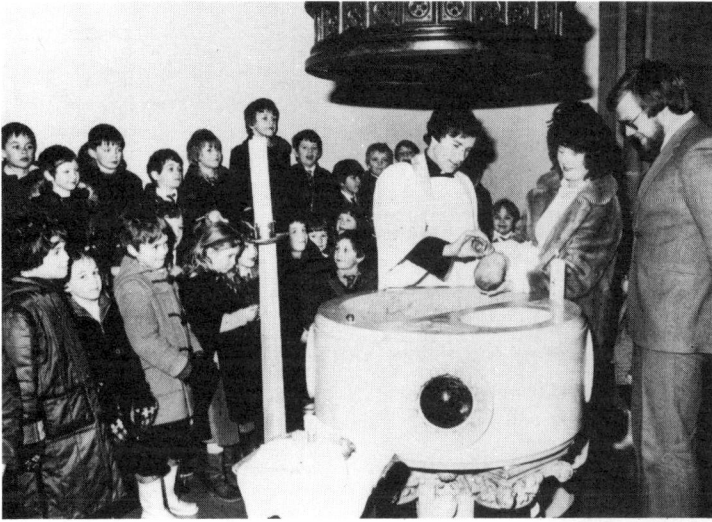

A personal milestone
Here children from St Wilfrid's Primary School,
York attend the baptism of one of their
classmates' baby sister

Relationships
Jimmy Saville, a Radio and TV personality and a
committed Christian with the disabled at Stoke
Mandeville Hospital

A 20th century issue
Christians from different traditions
take the platform at
this Life Rally

5

ONE CHURCH: THREE TRADITIONS

What's in a Name?

Every Saturday our newspapers carry advertisements and news about what's on in town:

films shown in local cinemas;

discos in different night spots;

sporting events, such as football matches and hockey fixtures.

A lot of this information is also available on our T.V. screens by the teletext system.

So we can plan our weekends to make the most of our free time. We can also use this information to learn what others are doing. The activities advertised give clues about how other people spend their time. In turn, this tells us what events and happenings they think worthwhile.

To find out who the Christians are and what they think is important, we begin therefore with one particular group of advertisements, church notices. Each week many newspapers carry information about the different church services being held. Most of the people who go regularly to church on Sunday do not need to study the church notices as they are members of a local church which they attend week by week. Some, however, may be on holiday and are looking for a church in which to worship. Others may have moved into a new area and are searching around for a church to join. The church notices usually tell us the time of the service, the name of the person who is to conduct it, and sometimes even a list of meetings or other activities during the week.

Those who are interested in studying religion will find that the names of different churches give us further information. Many of them include the word 'Parish' in their title. In Scotland this is a clue that they belong to the national Church of Scotland. Others may include the words 'Our Lady' in their titles or be named after saints. This is often a clue that they belong to the Roman Catholic Church.

Other notices in the newspaper may invite you to worship with groups of Christians such as Methodists, Baptists, or Congregationalists. Throughout England, in city, town and village are churches of the Church of England (the Anglican Church). In Scotland the Episcopal Church follows a way of worship very similar to that of the Church of England. Wales and Ireland also have their national Churches.

One famous Church which you would not usually find in the weekly notices is the Orthodox Church. Its members usually belong to closely-knit communities and when visitors or immigrants arrive they find out about it from relatives or friends.

For our study, the various branches or denominations of the Christian Church can be grouped under three headings: Orthodox, Roman Catholic, Reformed. Such a grouping is brief and easy to remember, but it is not completely accurate.

CHURCH NOTICES

THE CATHEDRAL
The Fourth Sunday after Easter
11 a.m. The Kirking of the Lord Provost. Bailies. and Councillors of the City of Glasgow.
The Rev William J. MORRIS. LLd. DD.
6.30 p.m. Evening Service
The Rev FERGUS C. BUCHANAN. MA. BD. Music:
11 a.m. Ps. 65: Kommit. eilet und laufet—Bach
6.30 p.m. Stanford in A; erschallet Ihr Himmel — Bach.

ADELAIDE PLACE BAPTIST CHURCH
(corner of Pitt Street and Bath Street)
11 a.m. — Leadership in the Church (2)
7 p.m. — Baptismal service.
Rev. DONALD P. McCALLUM
All welcome to these services

BALSHAGRAY PARISH CHURCH
Broomhill Cross
11 a.m.—Rev. R. STEWART FRIZZELL. B.D.
Parade of Uniformed Organisations

BELHAVEN WESTBOURNE
11 a.m. and 3 p.m.
Holy Communion
The Rev D. JOHNSTONE. M.C..B.D.
Retiring collection for mission and service fund.
Today Spring Fayre in Westbourne Gardens. (weatherpermitting) to be opened at 2 p.m. by Mr Johnny Beattie. Stalls. Teas available in church hall. All welcome.

BROOM CHURCH
Rev. NEILSON PETERKIN. M.A.
10 a.m. — First Service
Junior and Senior Sunday Schools
Junior Bible Class
10.40 a.m. —
"The Coffee Break"
11.30 a.m. —
Second Service
Creche. Nursery and Primary Sunday School
12.30 p.m. — Senior Bible Class and First Communicants Class
Wednesday 10.30 a.m. — "Wednesday Break"

BROOMHILL CHURCH
RANDOLPH ROAD
Rev JAMES AITCHISON. M.A..B.D.
11 a.m. and 6.30 p.m. the minister.

CATHCART OLD PARISH
CARMUNNOCK ROAD
11 a.m. — Service of Praise Led by the Linn choir and the Highfield Male Voice Choir.
6.30 p.m. — Evening Service.
Rev ALEX T. STEWART. M.A..B.D.
and Rev JOHN A. MacDONALD. M.A.
Creche provided.
All welcome.

CATHCART SOUTH CHURCH
Rev GEORGE FAIRLIE. B.D. B.V.M.S.
9.30 a.m. Morning Worship
10.15 a.m. Coffee Break
11 a.m. Morning Worship
Sacrament of Baptism.

CATHOLIC CHURCH
Garnetbank Primary School.
Garnthill
Tomorrow. Sunday
6.30 p.m.
Traditional Latin Mass

CROSSHILL QUEEN'S PARK PARISH CHURCH
40 Queen's Drive
11 a.m. — Mr Ian Matheson. B.Mus.

DRUMCHAPEL OLD PARISH CHURCH
Rev. DAVID A. KEDDIE. M.A..B.D.
11 a.m. — Morning Service
6.30 p.m. — Evening Service

EPISCOPAL CHURCH IN SCOTLAND
ST. MARGARET'S. NEWLANDS
8 a.m., 9.15 a.m., 12 noon: Holy Communion
11 a.m. The RECTOR
6.30 p.m. Mr JOHN MUIR

FREE PRESBYTERIAN CHURCH OF SCOTLAND
ST JUDES
137 Woodlands Road
11 a.m. and 6.30 p.m.
Rev. D. MacLEAN

HARPER MEMORIAL BAPTIST CHURCH
Craigiehall Street, Glasgow
Missionary Gift Day
Sunday 11 a.m. and 6.30 p.m.
The Rev BURTON SCOTT
Missionary Display of Work
Monday 7.30 p.m.
Speaker Miss M. Wilson, Qua Iboe Mission
All Welcome

GIFFNOCK SOUTH PARISH CHURCH
EASTWOOD TOLL
11.15 a.m. and 3 p.m.
Sacrament of the Lord's Supper
6.30 p.m. Thanksgiving Service
7.30 p.m. Intercession for the sick

GLASGOW UNIVERSITY CHAPEL
11 a.m.—
Settlement Sunday
Rev. L. A. RITCHIE. M.A..B.D.
Chaplain
Preacher—
The Rev. Professor JAMES BARR. M.A. B.D. Professor of Hebrew. in the University of Oxford.
Anthem—Almighty and Everlasting God. (Orlando Gibbons).

GREENBANK PARISH CHURCH
(Clarkston)
11 a.m. — Morning Worship
Mr JOHN VERNAL. D.A.
3 p.m. — Senior and Junior Sunday Schools. Promotion Service.
6.30 p.m. — No Evening Service at Greenbank. Christian Aid Dedication Service at Netherlee Parish Church.
All Cordially Welcome

HILLHEAD BAPTIST CHURCH
(Cresswell Street off Byres Road)
11.0 a.m.—Christian Aid Service.
6.30 p.m.—Evening Service.
Dramatic Reading by students of RSAMD.
Rev. W. EDWARD FRASER. M.A.. B.D.
All welcome.

HYNDLAND PARISH CHURCH
Fourth Sunday after Easter
11 a.m.
Rev. J. A. MACNAUGHTON. B.D.
Sacrament of Holy Communion at close of service.

JORDANHILL PARISH CHURCH
Woodend Drive
11 a.m. Mr. J.G. WILLIAM-SON
7 p.m. Video-recording of Easter Service
Creche available at morning service

KELVINSIDE, HILLHEAD Parish Church
11 a.m.—Morning Worship
Confirmation and admission.
Kirk Session meets at 10.30 a.m.
Rev. G. M. DENNY GRIEVES. M.A.. B.D.
Monday. 10th May
Kirk session meets at 7.30 p.m. and Congregational Board at 8.15 p.m.

KINGS PARK PARISH CHURCH
242 Castlemilk Road
10 a.m. and 11.15 a.m.
The Rev. G. STEWART SMITH. M.A. B.D.. S.T.M.
6.30 p.m. — "Carols for Christian Aid" led by junior choir and youth fellowship.

LANSDOWNE PARISH CHURCH.
KELVINBRIDGE
11 a.m.—Morning Service.
Rev. J. L. MILLER. M.A..B.D.
Congregational board meets Thursday. 13th May at 7.30 p.m.

MERRYLEA PARISH CHURCH
11 a.m. — Morning Service
Rev. SIDNEY H. COLEMAN. B.A.. B.D.. M.Th.
Sunday Schools meet as usual. Creche available.

NETHERLEE PARISH CHURCH
Ormonde Drive
11 a.m. — Morning Service
6.30 p.m. — Joint Service for Christian Aid Week
Rev. A. D. K. ARNOTT. M.A.. B.D.

NEW KILPATRICK PARISH CHURCH. BEARSDEN
The Rev. DAVID S.M. HAMILTON
The Rev. RALPH C.P. SMITH
11.30 a.m. and 6.30 p.m.
Holy Communion
(Creche in New Halls during 11.30 Service)

NEWLANDS (SOUTH)
11.15 a.m. and 6.30 p.m.
Rev. ALWYN J. C. MACFARLANE. M.A.
and Rev. G. FRASER H. MACNAUGHTON. B.D.
All most welcome.
Sunday Schools and Bible Class meet at usual times.

NEWTON MEARNS PARISH CHURCH
9.30 a.m.. 11.30 a.m.. and 3 p.m. Communion
6.30 p.m. — Service of Thanksgiving preceded by short Communion Service.
Rev. GRAHAM R. G. CARTLIDGE. M.A.. B.D.. S.T.M.

NORTH KELVINSIDE CHURCH
Queen Margaret Drive
Rev. W. G. ALSTON
Services 11 a.m. and 7 p.m.
Prayer Meeting 6.30 p.m.

OLD PARTICK PARISH CHURCH
11 CHURCH STREET. G11
11 a.m. — Rev JOHN JOLLY. B.A. and Mr ANDREW JOLLY. B.D.
Student assistant. Linthouse St. Kenneth's.

ORCHARDHILL PARISH CHURCH.
Church Road. Giffnock.
11 a.m. and 6.30 p.m.—
Rev. JOHN M. SPIERS. L.Th.
10.45 a.m.—Creche.
Sunday Schools and Bible Classes meet at usual times.
7.30 p.m.—Youth Fellowship. A.G.M.

RENFIELD ST STEPHENS PARISH CHURCH
260 Bath Street
11 a.m.—Rev. J. STEWART. M.A..B.D.
Boys Brigade and Girls Brigade parading.
All welcome to kirk lunch.
6.30 p.m.—Rev. A. TURNER. M.A..B.D.
Visitors most welcome.

SANDYFORD HENDERSON MEMORIAL CHURCH
13 Kelvinhaugh Street. Glasgow G3.
Rev. GEORGE M. PHILIP. M.A.
11 a.m. — Studies in 2nd Chronicles
6.30 p.m. — Studies in Luke's Gospel
7.30 p.m. (Tonight Sat.) — Bible Story and Prayer Meeting

SHERBROOKE ST GILBERT'S CHURCH
240 Nithsdale Road
Rev JOHN CAMPBELL. B.A.. L.Th.
Mr JAMES McNAUGHTAN. B.D.
11 a.m. Creche available.

ST GEORGE'S-TRON PARISH CHURCH
(Buchanan Street)
Rev ERIC J. ALEXANDER and Rev WILLIAM DUNLOP
11 a.m. and 3 p.m. Sacrament of the Lord's Supper
7 p.m. Evening Service Rev ERIC J. ALEXANDER
Wednesday at 7.30 p.m. House Groups
Visitors welcome

ST JOHN'S RENFIELD CHURCH
(Beaconsfield Road. G12)
9.30 a.m. and 11 a.m.—Morning Worship
Rev. COLIN G. McINTOSH. M.A.. B.D.
A retiring collection will be taken on behalf of Christian Aid.

STRATHBUNGO
QUEEN'S PARK CHURCH
(170 Queen's Drive. G42)
Rev. NORMA STEWART. M.A.. M.Ed.. B.D.
11 a.m.—Studies in Deuteronomy.
6.30 p.m.—Letters to the Churches (6)

ENGLISH EPISCOPAL CHURCH OF ST. SILAS
Park Road. Kelvinbridge
11 a.m. — Morning Prayer
Rev. M. CLANCY
6.30 p.m. — Series 3. Holy Communion
Rev. M. EVANS

SHAWLANDS CROSS CHURCH
The Church at the Cross
Rev. ALASTAIR M. SANDERSON. B.A.. L.Th.
11.15 a.m. — Ordination of Elders
6.30 p.m. — Evening Service

UNITARIAN CHURCH
287 St Vincent Street
Worship 11 a.m.
Rev. JOHN CLIFFORD

VISIT TO GLASGOW
of
Rev. DAVID PAWSON
Monday 10th May and Tuesday 11th May. at 7 30 p.m.
Govan Town Hall
Summertown Road
Come and hear God's Message for today.

WELLINGTON CHURCH
University Avenue
11 a.m. Rev. JOHN A. GRIMSON. M.A.
7 p.m. Rev. MAXWELL CRAIG. B.D.. Th.M.

WILLIAMWOOD CHURCH
11 a.m. — Rev. COLIN CAMPBELL. M.A.. B.D.

JOCK TROUP MEMORIAL CHURCH
(Tent Hall Fellowship)
Meeting at Adelphi Secondary School, Commercial Road, off Ballater Street.
SPECIAL TONIGHT 7 p.m.
"THE COUNTERFEIT COMING OF A COUNTERFEIT CHRIST"
A special address exposing the rec t announcement that Jesus Christ had come back arth and is due to make a TV appearance.
The coming again of Jesus Christ — what the Bible says
SUNDAY SERVICES
11 a.m. — MORNING WORSHIP
7 p.m. — GOSPEL SERVICE
THURSDAY 2 p.m. — WOMEN'S OWN MEETING (City Hall, Albion Street.)
7.30 — BIBLE STUDY/PRAYER MEETING
Everyone very welcome
For God and Scotland
(N.B. See additional notice about the Papal visit)

PROTESTANT AND CONSTITUTIONALIST PARADE AND RALLY AGAINST THE PROPOSED PAPAL VISIT
SATURDAY, 22nd MAY
PARADE LEAVING BLYTHSWOOD SQUARE, 10.30 a.m. prompt
(assemble 10 a.m.)
Public rally Bellahouston Park, 11.45 a.m. (approx).
Speakers include:
Dr Ian R. K. Paisley, MP, Belfast.
Rev Brian Green, London.
Rev David Cassells, Glasgow.
This will be the last chance to make a public witness against the Papal visit before the arrival of the Pope in the UK.
If the visit is cancelled, the event will continue as a thanksgiving demonstration. Surely everyone can see by now the intentions of the Papacy in this visit.
Come join with us!
Bus parties can be facilitated.
Ministers invited to lead the parade.
Further information: British Council of Protestant Christian Churches, care of 36 Deanwood Avenue. Glasgow G44 3RJ. Telephone 041 637 6166.

Reformed Churches

Our problem comes with the third group: Reformed. The large number of Churches grouped under Reformed, sometimes called 'Protestant', have many different practices and ways of organizing themselves. Some Churches in the Reformed group, for example, see themselves as having more in common with the Roman Catholic Church than with some of the other 'Protestant' Churches. The boundary lines cannot be drawn too rigidly.

Even within one denomination there may be a wide range of beliefs and practices. Within the large Anglican Church, for example, some members feel that they have a great deal in common with the Methodist Church and perhaps hope for a future coming together of these two traditions. Other Anglican members feel more at home with the form of worship of the Roman Catholic Church.

In a book of this size, it is not possible to study all the different Reformed Churches in detail. We will focus our attention on The Church of Scotland, which highlights some of the features of Reformed Churches.

The Ecumenical Movement

In recent years the different branches of the Christian Church have been worshipping and working more closely together internationally, nationally, and at a local level. This is part of what is known as The Ecumenical Movement, a sign of the unity and co-operation of the worldwide Church.

Some Christians hope that the different denominations will come together to form one organized Church. Others wish to maintain their own traditions while developing close links with other traditions.

A Church of Scotland in Linlithgow commemorates the Pope's visit to Britain in 1982

TEST YOUR UNDERSTANDING

- Study the church notices in this week's newspaper. How many are there?
- How many notices tell you the denomination of the church?
- Which denominations have notices in the paper?
- Most of those which do not state their denomination belong to the national church. Which church is this? (Note that your answer will depend on which part of the United Kingdom you live in.)
- Which notice gives you most information? Make a note of what it says.
- Which notice do you find most interesting? Explain why.

Two Thousand Years of Christianity

Why are there different branches of the Christian Church? To answer this we have to go back to the beginning of Christianity. The word 'Christian' comes from the title 'Christ' which means 'anointed one'. In ancient times Jewish kings went through a special ceremony in which they were anointed with oil, that is, some oil was sprinkled on their heads. Later, when the Jews no longer had a king of their own, the title was used to describe the great leader they believed God would send them. Their hope was that he would lead them to conquer their enemies and bring them a new and prosperous way of life in their own beloved land.

Around two thousand years ago, some Jews gave this title 'Christ' to Jesus of Nazareth, a teacher from a country village. Jesus was crucified, that is, put to death on a cross. But his followers came to believe that God had raised him from the dead. This was taken as the final sign that Jesus was the 'Christ'. The message of these early Christians, as the first followers of Jesus came to be called, was a startling one. They called it the Gospel, or Good News. The long-awaited new way of life had arrived. To use their language: 'God's Kingdom' had begun. But it was not to be for the Jews alone. It was for people of every country who put their trust in God and became followers of Jesus.

Within thirty years of Jesus' death on the cross, the early Christians had preached the story and meaning of the life, death and resurrection of Jesus all over the Mediterranean world. They carried the Gospel as far as Rome, the capital city of the Roman Empire. It was there that two great followers of Jesus, Peter and Paul, were put to death about A.D. 65. The history of the Christian Church was one of persecution and suffering for the next two and a half centuries.

The Conversion of Constantine

In the year A.D. 306, however, when the Emperor died, the Roman troops in York adopted his son Constantine who was their army commander, as their new Emperor. He fought his way across Europe to subdue the whole Roman Empire. A famous legend tells that he had a vision of a burning cross in the sky with the words: 'In this sign conquer'. So Constantine was converted to Christianity and he took the Chi-Rho symbol as the sign to be used on his battle standards. The Chi-Rho symbol is made from the first two letters of the Greek word for 'Christ' and together they form a cross.

Until that time, as we have seen, Christianity had been largely a forbidden and persecuted religion. Now, by the command of Constantine, it was recognized

The stone carving 'The Trophy of the Cross' shows the Chi-Rho symbol contained within a laurel wreath which was the Roman sign of victory

as the religion of the Empire. Christians could worship legally and their meeting-places were free from attack. Constantine eventually moved his capital to the East, to the city which came to be known as Constantinople (now Istanbul in Turkey). Though certain other cities were important centres of Christianity, the two most powerful centres were to be Rome and Constantinople.

East and West

Over the centuries differences developed between the Churches in the West, which looked to Rome for guidance, and those in the East, which followed the traditions of Constantinople. Communication between East and West was difficult, and they were far apart. Political upheavals created barriers which made travel very difficult, and there was also the barrier of language. The West spoke Latin, the East spoke Greek.

It was not until the year A.D.1054, however, that a formal split took place. The Church was divided into two main branches: the Roman Catholic Church in the West, under the bishop or Pope of Rome, and the Orthodox Church in the East, based on Constantinople and ruled by its bishop or Patriarch.

Members of the Orthodox Church were to suffer greatly for their faith, from Muslim invaders and even at the hands of their fellow Christians from the West. In the 13th century, for example, the Crusaders of the West captured Constantinople and vandalized the splendid church there, tearing down its altar and destroying its furnishings. Christian East and Christian West were now deeply divided and became strangers to one another.

The Reformation

Five hundred years after the split between East and West, the Church in the West itself became divided as a result of the Reformation which swept through Western Europe in the 16th century. The Reformation was in part a protest against the power of the Pope and the wealth and corruption of the Church of that age. It was also mixed up with a political struggle in each of the countries involved and the rise of a new spirit of independence among ordinary people.

The Extent of Holy Roman
Empire about AD 362

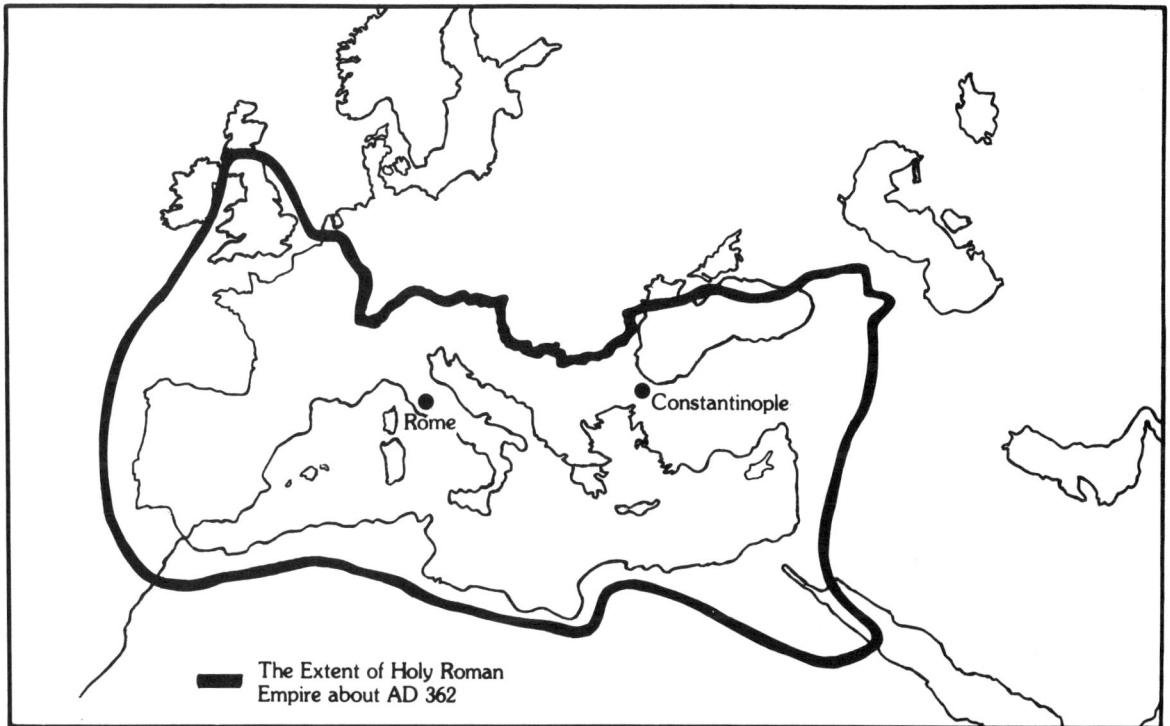

The Reformation brought about new forms of the Church in different countries, led by such men as Martin Luther in Germany and John Calvin in Switzerland. It also produced a counter-Reformation in the Roman Catholic Church which awoke that Church to its own reforms and to new missionary efforts.

In Scotland, the most famous name of the Reformation was John Knox. He was a follower of John Calvin and claimed that in Geneva he had seen 'The most perfect school of Christ that ever was in the earth since the days of the Apostles.' Knox and his fellow-reformers tried to establish the same pattern in their native Scotland.

The spirit of independence and freedom which was characteristic of the Reformation led to the growth of a large number of different 'Protestant' denominations, all loosely grouped together under the heading: The Reformed Church.

TEST YOUR UNDERSTANDING

- Study the picture of The Trophy of the Cross on page 10. What is the meaning of the stone carving?
- What advantages do you think the Church would get from Christianity becoming the official religion of the Roman Empire?
- Can you think of any possible disadvantages?
- Explain why Rome and Constantinople each became important centres of Christianity.
- What barriers made communication difficult between the Eastern and Western Churches?
- What do you think are the main barriers which separate Churches today?

Patriarch, Pope, Moderator

What are the similarities and differences between the various branches of the Church?

Though there are some important differences of belief and practice, all the main Churches of Christianity accept the Nicene Creed. Similarly, although there may be differences on some moral issues, such as divorce, all the Churches agree that the teaching of Jesus is the basis for what they believe about right and wrong.

The main difference we will look at is concerned with ways of worship. Before this, however, it is important to see how the various Churches are organized.

The Orthodox Church

The Orthodox Church is made up of a family of self-governing churches, each with its own Patriarch or bishop. Though all the bishops are equal, the Patriarch of Constantinople is still regarded as 'the first among equals' because of the importance of Constantinople in former days. The bishops are thought to be the true successors of the apostles, that is, the first followers of Jesus. It is their special task to safeguard and teach the Tradition of the Church.

Priests are responsible for the regular services of worship and for the sacraments of the Church. Sacraments are special actions through which Christians believe they receive God's help in their day-to-day lives. Before becoming a priest, an Orthodox Christian must first spend some time as a deacon. The deacon assists the priest in all the duties of worship. Married men are accepted as deacons and may become priests, though not bishops.

When a bishop or priest or deacon is ordained, that is, when he is set apart to take up his new work, the congregation has an important part to play in the service. At one point they are asked for their approval, and everyone shouts out: 'He is worthy!' to show that they agree.

The Orthodox Church can be found in Greece and Russia and many parts of Eastern Europe today. One word is a key to the Orthodox Church. It is the word 'Tradition'. One of their great teachers said: 'We keep the Tradition, just as we received it.'

Patriarchs and archbishops from different Orthodox churches worship together

The Roman Catholic Church

The Roman Catholic Church is the largest Christian body in the world. Roman Catholics believe that St Peter was the leader and first bishop of the Church in Rome. St Peter came to be regarded as the keeper of the gate of heaven, his symbol being a key or bunch of keys. That is why crossed keys appear in the Pope's emblem as a sign of his authority. As successor to Peter, the Pope is called 'the vicar of Christ, head of the bishops, and supreme governor of the whole Catholic Church'.

To support their views on the authority of the Church, Roman Catholics quote the words of Jesus:

'I tell you, Peter: you are a rock, and on this rock foundation I will build my church, and not even death will ever be able to overcome it. I will give you the keys of the Kingdom of heaven; what you prohibit on earth will be prohibited in heaven, and what you permit on earth will be permitted in heaven.'

(Matthew 16: 18-19)

The three major Orders of the Roman Catholic Church are: the bishops, the priests, and the deacons. There are many other ranks in the vast and highly-organized Roman Catholic Church, for example, the cardinals, who are the advisers of the Pope in matters affecting the worldwide government of the Church. Probably the best-known figure is the parish priest, whose tasks include conducting the service of the Mass and being responsible for the sacraments.

From time to time the Roman Catholic Church has called Councils to state clearly what the Church believes, to exert authority over the lives of its members, and to deal with wrong-doing or heresy (wrong belief). On the whole, the Roman Catholic Church has always been marked by its respect for authority. So *dogma,* that is, doctrine or belief laid down by authority, has been the important word in the long history of the Church.

The Second Vatican Council met in 1962 to further Christian unity. Over 2500 bishops from all over the world attended. Pope John XXIII is enthroned at the far end.

Pope John Paul II

The Church of Scotland

The Church of Scotland is a Presbyterian church. The term 'Presbyterian' refers to the Churches which work through self-governing elected courts. The emphasis in these Churches is on the importance and responsibility of all members of the Church.

The work of the Church of Scotland is dealt with by various courts, ranging from the Kirk Session elected by each congregation, to the General Assembly which meets once a year and has the final say on spiritual or religious issues affecting the Church.

The Kirk Session is made up of elders, both men and women, together with the minister of the parish who acts as chairman. Elders are elected by the members of the congregation. It is the duty of the elders to take an interest in any religious issue which arises in the parish, that is, the local area surrounding their church. They also supervise the activities of the congregation and help the minister in conducting the sacrament known as Holy Communion. Elders normally hold office for life.

Like the elders, the minister is chosen and elected by the congregation. His particular duties are to preach, which means to explain the teaching of the Bible, and to conduct the sacraments of Baptism and Holy Communion. The minister also conducts marriages and funerals, helps with some of the organizations run by his church, and visits members of his congregation, especially the old and the sick. Every part of Scotland is divided into parishes and all who live in the parish are entitled to the services of the minister when required, whether they are members of the Church or not. For convenience we have referred to the minister as 'he' but women may also be ordained as ministers.

Right Rev Dr J. Fraser McLuskey in the traditional dress of Moderator of the General Assembly of the Church of Scotland

The General Assembly of the Church of Scotland meets every year in Edinburgh in the month of May. It is made up of an almost equal number of ministers and elders from churches throughout Scotland. The chairman is a minister who is given the title Moderator of the General Assembly, and during his year as Moderator he travels widely in Scotland and abroad as the official representative of the Church. The General Assembly discusses issues of local, national and international interest whether they concern the welfare of Scotland or of its national Church. When the need arises, the General Assembly introduces rules which it believes are for the good of the Church.

TEST YOUR UNDERSTANDING

- Explain in you own words the following terms: apostles, ordained, sacraments.
- In the Orthodox Church, who are regarded as the successors of the apostles?
- In the Roman Catholic Church, why are keys included in the Pope's emblem?
- What are the responsibilities of the Moderator of the General Assembly of the Church of Scotland? For how long does he hold office?
- Suggest one advantage and one disadvantage of each of these systems of Church organization.

Research

- Interview your local priest or minister and prepare a report on a typical week in his working life.

CHRISTIANS
AT WORSHIP

3

Worship in Church

Places of Worship

Christians can worship anywhere – in private houses, hospitals, schools, prisons, or out in the open air. But travel anywhere in the world today, and wherever you find Christians able to worship freely, you will come across church buildings. All through the centuries, church buildings have been designed and built by Christians from every branch of the Church.

One reason for having special places of worship is that they are signs to others – 'public statements', if you like, of Christian belief and practice. Study these pictures of churches, and also look at the churches you pass going to and from school. Where there are notice boards, these will often give a picture of the life of the church. But look carefully at the building itself – its shape, its windows, carvings, statues, or any other special features. What clues do they give about the beliefs of those who worship there?

Once inside the church we discover the main reason why Christians worship in special buildings. Places of worship are carefully designed so that their shape, size, decorations and furnishings help people in their worship. By exploring church buildings, therefore, we can find clues to how Christians worship and what they believe about the meaning and purpose of life.

Priest and People

In some traditions, and especially at certain periods in the past, worship has been regarded as an activity to be 'performed' by priests and their helpers in front of an 'audience' who watched what was happening, but took no active part in the performance itself. Also, although the congregation could see what was happening, often the words could not be heard. Even if they were, they were in a foreign language which ordinary people could not understand. Often the priests and other Church officials were separated from the congregation, behind a screen. In the eyes of ordinary people this gave the churchmen more status. The mysteries and secrets of religion were entirely in their hands.

In other traditions, and generally throughout the Western Church today, the emphasis is on 'corporate' or 'congregational' worship in which all the people can be seen to play an active part in the service.

This may take many forms: singing hymns, repeating the Lord's Prayer together, reciting the Creed, and taking Communion. Because everyone is involved, there is less separation between the priest and the congregation. In some modern churches the building is either square or round and the priest or minister leads the worship from the centre. This emphasizes the idea that he (or she) is in the midst of the people and not separated from them. So every member has an important part to play in the worship of the Church.

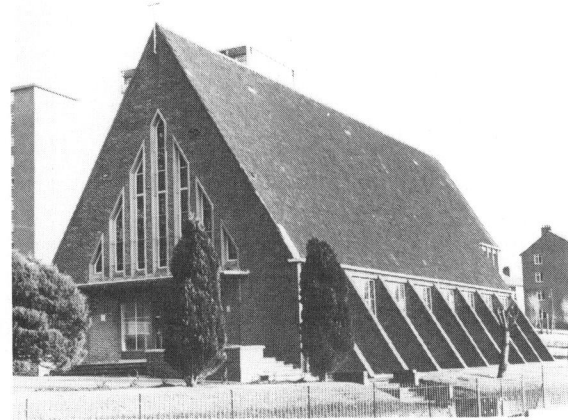

Multi-purpose Churches

Many Christians today see the role of the church building not only as providing a special place for holding services of worship, but also as a centre for such things as discussions and debates, performances of concerts or plays, a meeting-place for youth clubs and many other activities.

One answer to this in recent years has been the multi-purpose church. Though these take different forms, one pattern is where the main part of the building is used for worship only on Sundays, Saints' days and festivals. The rest of the time it is available for meetings and other activities. All the furniture and furnishings have, of course, to be movable. For Christians who have always thought of their church as 'dedicated' or set apart from all ordinary affairs, this raises important questions both about the nature of worship and the role of the church.

A hive of activity in a community church

Patterns of Worship

If you go along to the morning service in a local church for two or three weeks you will find that what the minister or priest and the congregation do together follows a certain pattern. You will hear the same or similar prayers and hymns and see the same rituals or special actions. If you then go to a church belonging to another denomination, there is a good chance that you will recognize a similar pattern and hear some of the very same prayers and hymns.

The pattern of worship which a Church follows is known as the liturgy. Though there are many differences in what you see and hear during Orthodox, Roman Catholic and Church of Scotland worship which we will look at in turn, there is a common pattern behind each of their liturgies.

In the first half of each service the centre of attention is the teaching of the Bible. That is why this part is known as 'The Liturgy of the Word'. In the second part of the service the centre of attention is what is done at the altar or Communion Table. So this part is called: 'The Liturgy of the Eucharist, or Holy Communion.' The word Eucharist comes from a Greek word meaning 'thanksgiving'.

As we shall see, most congregations of the Church of Scotland do not celebrate Holy Communion every week, but at every Sunday morning service the minister receives the offerings of the people at the Holy Table. This reminds the worshippers that the Holy Table is the focus for everyone in the church. It is to the Table that the offerings of bread and wine are brought at the full service of Holy Communion in remembrance of the Last Supper and the death of Christ.

TEST YOUR UNDERSTANDING

- Suggest two reasons why Christians worship in special buildings.
- Why are there similarities and differences between church buildings belonging to different traditions?
- If a church is divided into two parts by a screen, what may this tell us about how worship is conducted in that church?
- Why are some modern church buildings square or round?
- Make a list of activities which you think it would be all right to hold in a church.

1

Research

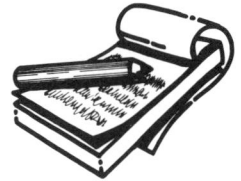

- Conduct a survey to find out why people go to church. One way of doing this is to draw up a list of reasons and use it as a basis for a questionnaire. Leave some space on the questionnaire so that people can add reasons of their own. If you intend to use the survey in a local church, make sure that you get the permission of the minister or priest beforehand.

Places of Worship

The Orthodox Church

This is what you see and hear and take part in if you are a worshipper in an Orthodox Church.

The inside of an Orthodox Church is a picture gallery of the Orthodox faith. The walls and ceiling are covered with beautiful paintings and mosaics, each one prepared with prayer and devotion by the artist. The pictures of Jesus, often with Mary his mother, and the apostles and saints are called 'icons', a Greek word which means 'likeness' or 'image'.

All Orthodox churches have an icon screen, usually of wood, with icons painted on the panels. The icon screen divides the sanctuary from the main body of the church. The church is usually in the shape of a square, or of a cross, with a wide central space covered by a dome. There are usually no pews or seats in this central part, and the worshippers stand or move about during the service. They feel at home in their church, for worship is a family affair. They are 'children in their Father's house'.

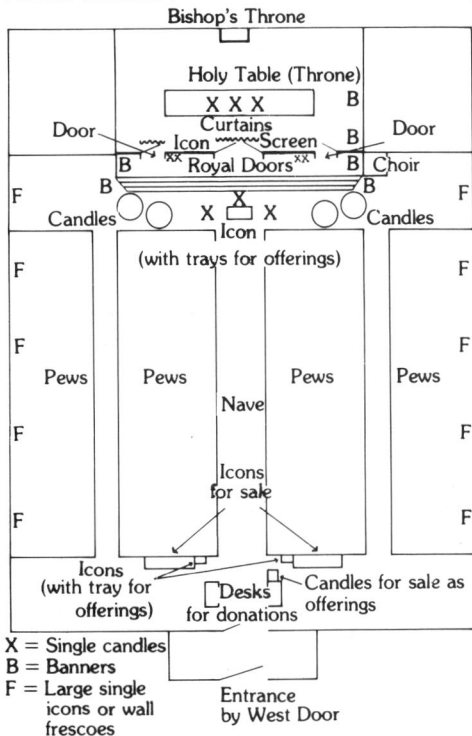

Bishop's Throne

Holy Table (Throne)

X X X — B

Door — Curtains

Icon — Screen — B — Door

B — Royal Doors — B — Choir

F — B — B — F

Candles — X — X — Candles

Icon

(with trays for offerings)

F — F

F — F

Pews — Pews — Pews — Pews

Nave

F — F

Icons for sale

F — F

Icons (with tray for offerings)

Desks for donations — Candles for sale as offerings

X = Single candles
B = Banners
F = Large single icons or wall frescoes

Entrance by West Door

Interior of St. George's Serbian Orthodox Church, Leicester and groundplan (courtesy of P.T. Emmett, R.E. Centre, Leicester). This particular church has pews where worshippers sit for the sermon as it has been adapted from a former Anglican building

In the middle of the icon screen there is a double door known as the Royal Doors or the Holy Door. When it is open, at certain parts of the service, the worshipper can see the altar – known as the Holy Table or Throne – in the sanctuary. Behind the table is the bishop's throne.

The worshipper enters the church, buys a candle, lights it and puts it in a candlestick in front of an icon. He crosses himself and kisses the icon. The nave, or main part of a church, fills with worshippers. Men and women usually stand separately.

The ritual of the service involves both priests and people. There is a continual repetition of prayers and to each petition the choir and people respond: 'Kyrie eleison' which means: 'Lord, have mercy'. They make the sign of the cross and bow in reverence. The whole service is sung or chanted without the help of any musical instruments. The singing is deep and splendid, and the smoke of incense fills the air with a sharp sweetness.

Because of their common background, the special clothes or vestments worn by the Orthodox priest during the service of the Eucharist are much the same as those of the Roman Catholic Church, which we look at later. The clothes, however, are much more richly decorated and often embroidered in gold.

TEST YOUR UNDERSTANDING

- State in your own words what each of the following are: icons, icon screen, Holy Door.
- What does the phrase 'children in their Father's house' tell us about the Orthodox Christian's attitude to worship?

The Roman Catholic Church

This is what you see and hear and take part in if you are a worshipper in a Roman Catholic church.

The most important part of the Roman Catholic church is the sanctuary or holy place which is usually at the east end of the church. It reminds us that the Christian faith came to us from the East. The building is arranged in such a way that all the worshippers face the sanctuary, and it is there that most of the important features and furnishings are to be found.

The altar is the focal point of worship and it is here each day that the priest performs the most important act of Roman Catholic worship, the Mass. Roman Catholics believe that the bread and wine which are at the heart of the Mass become in a mysterious way the body and blood of Christ.

Some of the wafers of bread which are blessed during the service are always kept in the tabernacle, a decorated cupboard or box with a lock and key. Thus what Roman Catholics call the Blessed Sacrament is always present in the church. The sanctuary lamp, a light burning near the tabernacle, also reminds worshippers that in a special sense Jesus Christ can be found in the church at all times.

Within the sanctuary, and close to the altar, is the lectern at which the priest or a member of the congregation reads passages from the Bible during each service. It has been the custom in recent years for the sermon, or talk based on the Bible, to be preached from the altar area.

Early morning Mass in a modern Roman Catholic church

Another important piece of furniture in the church is the font. Water represents purity and new life, and it is through baptism that one becomes, usually as a very young baby, a member of the Church. You will also see a private room or rooms where Roman Catholics may make confession of their sins and ask God's forgiveness before they come to Mass.

The importance of light as a symbol to Christians is shown not only by the sanctuary lamp, but also by many candles. They are to be seen on the altar, and prominent in the church is a large stand which holds many candles. Roman Catholics will often light a candle as a symbol for prayer to thank God for some good which they have received or to ask his help for a friend or relative who may be ill or in trouble. Candles may also be found in front of statues of the Virgin Mary and of the saints.

On the walls of the church can be seen a series of fourteen pictures or carvings known as 'The Stations of the Cross'. These illustrate incidents from the last few hours of the life of Jesus. Especially in the days leading up to Easter, Roman Catholics use these pictures to help to guide their prayers and thoughts.

During the service of the Mass incense may be used as a mark of reverence, when the priest walks round the altar, then at the reading of the Gospel, and later when the holy gifts of bread and wine are brought to the altar for the Eucharist. The use of incense is a very ancient custom in worship and as the white sweet-smelling puffs rise in the air the people are reminded of a verse from the Psalms:

'I call to you, Lord; help me now!
Listen to me when I call to you.
Receive my prayer as incense.'

The priest who calls the people to worship and conducts the service wears special vestments or clothes which are set apart and blessed by the Church. His ordinary black gown is called a cassock, and it is simply his everyday dress or uniform.

When he is celebrating Mass, the priest wears the following vestments over his cassock:

the amice: an oblong piece of white linen with a cross sewn or embroidered on it and strings to fasten it round the shoulders.

the alb: a white linen tunic which reaches to the feet. It is a symbol of purity.

the cincture: a girdle worn round the waist to hold the alb in place.

the stole: a long narrow strip of cloth worn round the neck. It usually has three embroidered crosses, one at each end and one in the middle. The stole symbolizes the yoke of Christ.

the chasuble: the large outer garment which covers the others. The name comes from the Latin *casula* meaning 'a little house', because it shelters the priest from all evil. It may vary in colour depending on the season of the Christian year — white, red, rose, green, violet, black, gold or silver. The chasuble usually has a large cross embroidered on it.

A young R.C. priest wearing the green chasuble which he wears for most services

TEST YOUR UNDERSTANDING

● State in your own words what each of the following is: sanctuary, altar, tabernacle, Blessed Sacrament, sanctuary lamp, lectern, font, the Stations of the Cross.
● Explain why candles are to be found in Roman Catholic churches.

The Church of Scotland

This is what you see and hear and take part in if you are a worshipper in the Church of Scotland.

Every part of Scotland from the Shetland Islands to the Borders has a parish church of the Church of Scotland. The buildings take many forms. Some of them, especially in country districts, are small and very plain inside and outside, reminding us of the strictness and simplicity of the Presbyterian tradition. Others, especially in the new housing areas, are modern buildings which fit in well with their surroundings. But there are also noble and ancient churches such as St Mungo's church of Glasgow which is also known as Glasgow Cathedral, the Abbey of the Isle of Iona, and the High Church of Edinburgh, better known as St Giles.

The Church at work in every part of
Scotland

The Church of Scotland uses many of the same names for the parts and furnishings of the building – nave, aisles, lectern, pulpit – as we meet in churches of the other traditions which we have been exploring. But instead of speaking of the 'altar', the Church of Scotland uses the term 'Holy Table' or 'Communion Table'. It is still, however, in a central position, to be the focus of attention of all the worshippers. According to tradition the table will probably be bare and without elaborate decoration and will be made of stone or marble or, most often, of wood. For the service of Communion the table is covered with 'a white linen cloth'.

The Reformation in Scotland in the 16th century set out to simplify public worship, and we can see some of that influence in the churches of the nation to this day. A great deal that appealed to the senses – drama and vestments, lights and incense, paintings and statues, Latin prayers and choral chanting – disappeared from the Scottish parish church.

The Reformers stressed the importance of hearing a service and they put it into the language of the ordinary people. So the ear took the place of the eye in Scottish worship. Listening was more important than looking. The mind and the conscience were stressed at the expense of the emotions. The Word, that is, the Bible, was emphasized more than the mystery that surrounded Holy Communion.

So it came about that Bible readings, long prayers, and even longer sermons were the main features of Scottish worship for several centuries. Even the singing, in which the congregation joined, was limited to the Psalms. And for many years there were no organs, pianos or other musical instruments.

The church buildings were bare and free from any decoration, the main furnishings being pews and pulpit. Because of the importance of the Bible, churches were largely places for instruction and learning, and so the pulpit was often placed high in the centre of the wall which the worshippers attentively faced.

By tradition, the Bible and the Catechism – a collection of questions and answers about Christian beliefs – were the only Church books. The worshippers sat to pray and to listen to the reading of the Bible and stood only to sing the Psalms. Even the central Christian symbol of the cross was rare in the average Scottish parish church.

The simplicity of the building and of the service was reflected in the vestments of the minister, which remain simple to this day: his cassock, a black gown usually known as a Geneva gown, a hood from the University at which he studied, and white linen bands at his neck which symbolize the preaching 'gift of tongues'.

In recent times, however, the Church of Scotland has again come to understand the importance of symbol and ceremony in religion, a fact which the ancient cathedrals never lost. The Church is once more aware of the qualities which art and music, beautiful furnishings and proper ceremonial can bring to worship. So today there is organ music, hymns and choral singing, responsive prayer, the recital of Creeds, and a renewed emphasis on Holy Communion and the ceremony that surrounds the Communion Table.

A minister of the Church of Scotland wearing a stole over his Geneva gown

TEST YOUR UNDERSTANDING

- State in your own words what each of the following is: the Word, pulpit, Holy Table.
- Why are there fewer special actions and objects involved in Church of Scotland worship than in Orthodox and Roman Catholic worship?

Inside Cadder Parish Church, Bishopbriggs

Patterns of Worship

The Orthodox Church

A normal Sunday Eucharist in the Orthodox Church follows 'The Liturgy of St John Chrysostom' who was Patriarch of Constantinople in the 4th century. An outline of the service is:

The Preparation of the Bread and Wine
This is done by the priest or priests in the Chapel of Preparation, a small room to the left of the icon screen.

The Liturgy of the Word

The Litany of Peace
Litany is an ancient form of prayer which began in the Eastern Church. It consists of a series of petitions or short prayers sung or said by the priest. The choir and people respond with: *'Kyrie eleison'* – *'Lord, have mercy.'*

Psalm
'Hear my prayer, O Lord'. (Psalm 102).

Little Litany
The people respond: *'Kyrie eleison'* and make the sign of the cross.

The Beatitudes
The sayings of Jesus which start the Sermon on the Mount.

The Little Entrance
This is the procession where the priest brings in the Book of the Gospels, held high for everyone to see.

A Hymn for the Entrance

Trisagion
This is a prayer: *'Holy God, holy and mighty, holy and immortal, have mercy upon us'.* It is sung three or more times.

Readings from the Bible
From the Psalms
From the Epistles
From the Gospels

The Sermon

Prayers for the Church

cont.

The Liturgy of the Eucharist

The Great Entrance
A procession, led by the priest or priests, carrying the bread and wine in the holy vessels, accompanied by servers with candles and incense. As they pass through the worshippers in the church, the people bow in reverence. The Royal Doors are opened, and the priest goes through and lays the bread and wine on the Holy Table.

The Kiss of Peace and the Creed
The worshippers greet one another with the Kiss of Peace, and everyone recites the Nicene Creed.

Prayers of the Eucharist
Thanksgiving: Which ends with the Gospel story of the Last Supper, and the words of Christ:
'Take, eat, this is my body . . .
Drink of it, all of you, this is my blood . . .'
Remembrance: In which the priest calls to mind Christ's death and resurrection, and he offers the holy gifts of bread and wine to God.
Consecration: The prayer in which the priest calls down the Holy Spirit on the holy gifts.
Supplication, and The Lord's Prayer: 'Our Father . . .'

The Elevation and Fraction
The priest raises the consecrated bread for all to see and then breaks it into small pieces. The choir sings, and bells are rung.

The Communion of Priests and People
The priest comes and stands in front of the Royal Doors and those who are taking communion come forward to receive a piece of the holy bread dipped in wine and served on a spoon.

Thanksgiving and Final Blessing

The Antidoron
Everyone present comes up to kiss the cross which the priest holds, and to receive a small piece of bread, called the antidoron. It is shared as a sign of fellowship and love, like the meals the early Christians used to share together.

The Roman Catholic Church

Mass is the Roman Catholic name for the Eucharist or Holy Communion. We find the word in such festival names as Christmas, Candlemas, Martinmas.

Here is an outline of the Sunday Mass of the Roman Catholic Church as it is found in the Missal or book of service.

Preparation

The worshipper makes the sign of the cross on entering the church. He kneels for a few moments of quiet prayer, asking for the peace of God in his heart as he prepares for worship.

Entrance

As the priest and his servers make their way through the church towards the altar, the whole congregation sings a psalm or hymn. The priest kisses the altar and everyone makes the sign of the cross. Then the priest greets the people *'In the name of the Father, and of the Son, and of the Holy Spirit.'*

Penitential Rite

The people are encouraged to make confession of their sins in the presence of God. The priest tells them of God's forgiveness. The *Kyrie eleison* is repeated:

> *'Lord, have mercy.*
> *Christ, have mercy.*
> *Lord, have mercy.'*

Gloria

The *Gloria* is sung:

> *'Glory to God in the highest,*
> *and peace to his people on earth.'*

Collect

A short prayer is said by the priest on behalf of everyone and for the whole Church. It reminds the congregation of the theme for worship that day.

The Liturgy of the Word

Scripture Readings

From the Old Testament and the writings of the Apostles.

The Gospel

The priest makes the sign of the cross over the open page of the Gospel, then touches his forehead, lips and breast. The censer or incense-holder is swung at this point and the puffs of incense remind the worshippers of the importance of the Gospel.

Homily

A short sermon to build up the faith of the people.

cont.

Creed

All stand to say the Nicene Creed which unites everyone in the Church to think not about themselves, but of what God is and what he does.

Prayer of the Faithful

A prayer of intercession for all people, asking God's help for them.

The Liturgy of the Eucharist

The Preparation of the Gifts

The bread and wine for the Eucharist and gifts for the poor and for the Church are now brought in procession to the altar. The priest, following a traditional pattern of worship, places the paten or plate containing the bread and the chalice or cup of wine on the altar. He bows in prayer and asks that the gifts of bread and wine may be acceptable to God. The gifts and the altar may then be censed, i.e. have the incense swung over them. Next the priest washes his hands and invites the people to join with him in the prayer over the gifts.

The Eucharistic Prayer

This is the centre and high point of the service. The eight chief elements in the prayer are:

Thanksgiving

In the name of the entire people of God, the priest praises the Father and gives him thanks.

The Sanctus

All join together to sing or recite the Sanctus:

> Holy, holy, holy Lord, God of power and might,
> heaven and earth are full of your glory.
> Hosanna in the highest.
> Blessed is he who comes in the name of the Lord.
> Hosanna in the highest.

Invocation

The priest prays that the Holy Spirit will come upon the gifts of bread and wine to make them holy, 'so that they may become for us the body and blood of our Lord, Jesus Christ'.

The priest spreads his hands over the offerings of bread and wine as he prays.

Narrative and Elevation

The words from the Gospel which tell of the Last Supper in the upper room in Jerusalem on the night Jesus was betrayed. As he speaks the words of Consecration, the priest raises the bread and then the chalice for all to see. It is at the moment of Consecration that Roman Catholics believe the bread and wine on the altar are changed into the body and blood of Christ.

At the 'Elevation', as it is called, a bell is rung three times, and there is a moment of silent adoration. Incense reminds the worshippers of the holiness of this time in the service.

Memorial

The priest reminds the people of Christ, his death and resurrection, and what he has done for them. *'When we eat this bread and drink this cup, we proclaim your death, Lord Jesus, until you come in glory'*.

Offering

The priest reminds the people that the Mass is the same sacrifice as that of Calvary. Christ is truly present on the altar and is offered as *'a holy and living sacrifice'*.

Intercessions

Prayers for the whole body of the Catholic Church, for the Pope, for bishops and clergy everywhere, for *'those here present and all your people, and all who seek you with a sincere heart'*. The prayer includes all who have died *'in the peace of Christ and all the dead whose faith is known to you alone'*.

Doxology

The Eucharistic Prayer ends with the praise of God:

> *Through him*
> *with him*
> *in him*
> *in the unity of the Holy Spirit,*
> *all glory and honour is yours,*
> *almighty Father,*
> *for ever and ever,*
> AMEN.

The Lord's Prayer

This is said by everyone.

The Sign of Peace

The priest's prayer is: *'The peace of the Lord be with you always'*. People often shake hands with the worshippers who are next to them, or use some sign of goodwill.

The Breaking of Bread

The Breaking of Bread reminds everyone of the body of Christ broken on the cross. While the priest breaks the wafer of bread the congregation sings a very old chant of the Christian Church which is called *Agnus Dei*, literally, 'Lamb of God'.

'Lamb of God, you take away the sins of the world: have mercy upon us'.

The priest breaks off a small piece of the wafer and drops it in the chalice of wine.

Communion

First of all, the priest eats the bread and drinks some of the wine. Then the worshippers come up to the altar with their hands cupped to receive the wafer of bread or have it placed on their tongues.

The priest says: *'The body of Christ'* and, as the worshipper receives the wafer, each one says *'Amen'*.

cont.

Private Prayer
After communion the priest and people may spend some time in private prayer. They remind themselves that the word 'Eucharist' means 'thanksgiving'.

Blessing
The Service of the Mass ends with a Blessing:
'*May almighty God bless you, the Father, and the Son, and the Holy Spirit*'.
 Then the priest sends the people away with the words:
'*The Mass is ended, go in peace*'.

The Church of Scotland

In some congregations of the Church of Scotland the Sacrament of Holy Communion is held weekly, but in most churches Holy Communion is celebrated only three or four times a year. For the worshippers this emphasizes the solemnity and importance of the occasion. But even where Communion is a rare and special event in the Christian year, it gives shape to the ordinary Sunday morning service of worship.

 Here is an outline of the Service of Holy Communion in the Church of Scotland as it is set out in the Book of Common Order (1979) which is the guide to worship. Praise is usually from *The Church Hymnary,* Third Edition.

 At the hour when morning service begins, the church officer brings in the large Bible to the pulpit and opens it. Then he leads in the minister.

Preparation
The minister calls the congregation to worship, saying: '*Let us worship God*'.

Praise

Call to Prayer
The minister calls the people to prayer in words of the Bible, such as: '*O taste and see that the Lord is good. Blessed is the man that trusteth in him.*'

Prayers
Adoration:	a prayer of praise of the glory of God
Confession:	a prayer which says: '*We have sinned against thee in thought, word and deed*'.
Kyrie eleison:	'*Lord, have mercy, Christ, have mercy, Lord, have mercy.*'
Absolution:	a prayer asking God to forgive us.
Supplication:	a prayer asking for God's continuing help.

Praise

The Liturgy of the Word
Lesson from the Old Testament
Selected reading

Praise

The Epistle
Selected reading

The Gospel
Selected reading

Praise

Sermon
Ending with Ascription of Praise:
> *'Unto the Father, and unto the Son, and unto the Holy Spirit, be ascribed in the Church all honour and glory, might, majesty, dominion, and blessing, now and for ever. AMEN.'*

Praise

The Offering
The money collection for the work of the Church and for the poor is brought to the table at this time and dedicated to God.

Prayers of Intercession
> *'for thy one, holy, catholic and apostolic Church'*
> *'for this parish and congregation'*
> *'for our country, for thy servant Elizabeth our Queen, and all the royal family'*
> *'for all mankind'.*

The Liturgy of the Lord's Supper

The Invitation
> *'Beloved in the Lord, draw near to the holy table, and hear the gracious words of the Lord Jesus Christ'.*

Psalm
> *'Ye gates, lift up your heads on high'* (Metrical Psalm 24:7-10, *Church Hymnary* No. 566.)

During the singing of the Psalm the elements of bread and wine are brought into the church by the elders, and laid on the Holy Table.

The Nicene Creed
> *'I believe in one God, the Father Almighty . . .'*

The Grace
> *'The grace of the Lord Jesus Christ be with you all'.*

The Unveiling
The minister removes the white linen cloths which cover the bread and wine.

Prayer

Words of Institution
The words of St Paul: *'I have received of the Lord that which I also delivered unto you . . .'* (I Corinthians 11:23-6).

Consecration
'In the name of the Father, and of the Son, and of the Holy Spirit'.
Prayer of Consecration: including thanksgiving and the *Sanctus:*
   'Holy, holy, holy, Lord God of Hosts,
   Heaven and earth are full of thy glory . . .'
The Consecration of the bread and wine: *'that the bread which we break may be the communion of the body of Christ, and the cup of blessing which we bless the communion of the blood of Christ . . .'*

Prayers
For kindred and friends
For the sick and suffering
For the communion of saints.

The Lord's Prayer

The Breaking of Bread
   'Take, eat, this is my body which is broken for you: this do in remembrance of me'.

The Cup Is Raised
   'This cup is the new covenant in my blood: this do ye, as oft as ye drink it, in remembrance of me.'

Agnus Dei
   'Lamb of God, that takest away the sins of the world:
   Have mercy upon us.'

The Communion
The minister himself takes the bread and the wine. Then he gives the Holy Communion first to the elders beside him, then to the people, with the words:
   Take ye, eat ye; this is the body of Christ which is broken for you; this do in remembrance of him.
   'This cup is the new covenant in the blood of Christ, which is shed for many unto remission of sins; drink ye all of it.'

The Peace
   'The peace of the Lord Jesus Christ be with you all'.

Prayer of Thanksgiving
   'for this spiritual food . . .'

Praise

The Blessing
   'Go in peace; and the blessing of God Almighty, the Father, the Son and the Holy Spirit be upon you and remain with you always. AMEN.

Words of Praise

The following ancient words of praise are to be found in 'The Liturgy of the Eucharist or Holy Communion' in all the main branches of the Church:

Sursum corda

Minister/priest:	'Lift up your hearts'
People:	'We lift them up unto the Lord'
Minister/priest:	'Let us give thanks unto our Lord God'
People:	'It is meet and right so to do'

Sanctus: 'Holy, holy, holy, Lord God of Hosts, heaven and earth are full of thy glory: Glory be to thee, O Lord Most High.'

Agnus Dei 'Lamb of God, that takest away the sins of the world: Have mercy upon us. 'Lamb of God, that takest away the sins of the world: Have mercy upon us. 'Lamb of God, that takest away the sins of the world: Grant us thy peace.'

The Lord's Prayer Our Father, which art in heaven, Hallowed be Thy name: Thy kingdom come; Thy will be done; In earth as it is in heaven. Give us this day our daily bread. And forgive us our trespasses, as we forgive them that trespass against us. And lead us not into temptation; But deliver us from evil: For Thine is the kingdom, The power, and the glory, For ever and ever. AMEN.

(There is also an alternative version.)

The Nicene Creed 'I believe in one God the Father Almighty . . .' (see page 3)

_____ TEST YOUR UNDERSTANDING _____

● Prepare a table as shown below and use it to build up a summary of the service of worship followed by each tradition.

PATTERNS OF WORSHIP	ORTHODOX CHURCH	ROMAN CATHOLIC CHURCH	CHURCH OF SCOTLAND
Liturgy of the Word			
Liturgy of the Eucharist or Holy Communion			

What are the main similarities of the three ways of worship?

What are the main differences between the three ways of worship?

● People have five senses: sight, hearing, smell, taste, touch. Write a paragraph on each of the three traditions, showing how its way of worship takes account of the different senses.

──────────────────── *Research* ────────────────────

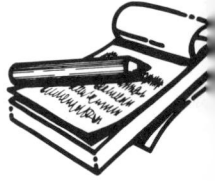

● This chapter has given you information on how some Christians worship, but as we have seen, it is important to 'see', 'hear' and 'take part in' worship really to get any insight into why Christians worship.

The best way to do this is to visit a local church. If the church belongs to one of the traditions we have looked at in this chapter, try to work out how the different parts of the service fit into the outline suggested in the previous pages.

● Services of worship are also broadcast on radio and television. Listen to one or two of these and record them if possible. Then compare them with what you have read about the liturgies.

Worship at Home

Christians worship not only in church and on Sundays or special days of festival. They are also encouraged to worship daily at home and on their own. Many are helped in this by the daily religious programmes on radio and television.

Though the private worship is set out here under the three main traditions we have been studying, many of the prayers and thoughts are used by Christians of all traditions.

Russian and Greek reli icons of the 17th centu

Orthodox

Orthodox Christians are guided in their private worship by special manuals which set down daily prayers for morning and evening, to be said in front of the icons in their own homes. Most of these prayers are taken from the service books used in public worship, so that even in their own homes Orthodox Christians feel they are joined together in prayer.

Instructions at the start of morning prayers stress the need to prepare oneself before beginning to pray:

'When you wake up, before you begin the day, stand with reverence before the All-Seeing God. Make the sign of the Cross and say: In the name of the Father, and of the Son, and of the Holy Spirit. AMEN.

Keep silence for a little, so that your thoughts and feelings may be freed from worldly cares . . .'

The following is an example of the morning prayer:

'O Lord, grant me to greet the coming day in peace. Help me in all things to rely upon Thy holy will. In every hour of the day reveal Thy will to me. Bless my dealings with all who surround me. Teach me to treat all that comes to me throughout the day with peace of soul, and with firm conviction that Thy will governs all. In all my deeds and words guide my thoughts and feelings. In unforeseen events let me not forget that all are sent by Thee. Teach me to act

firmly and wisely, without embittering and embarrassing others. Give me strength to bear the fatigue of the coming day with all that it shall bring. Direct my will, teach me to pray, pray Thou Thyself in me.   AMEN.'

Here are some phrases with which the evening prayers close:

'Forgive, O Lord, lover of men, those who hate and wrong us. Reward our benefactors. Grant to our brethren and friends all that they ask for their salvation and eternal life. Visit and heal the sick. Free the prisoners. Guide those at sea. Travel with those who travel . . .

Remember, O Lord, our departed parents and brethren and give them rest where shines the light of Thy face.'

The most famous of all Orthodox prayers is the Jesus Prayer:

'Lord Jesus Christ, Son of God, have mercy on me a sinner'.

This prayer is a source of strength to those who recite it continually and to those who use it only in times of particular need. Many Orthodox Christians use a rosary to help them to recite this prayer. The Orthodox rosary is made of wool, so that it makes no noise, unlike the string of beads which is the rosary of the Roman Catholic.

As well as saying their prayers, Orthodox Christians are encouraged to read the passages from the Epistle and the Gospel which are set down for the Church's worship each day of the year.

Roman Catholic

The best-known form of private worship in the Roman Catholic Church is the use of the Rosary. When a Catholic says the Rosary, he meditates on the life of Jesus and on the glory of heaven.

A rosary

Each part of the Rosary is devoted to a particular incident in the life of Jesus or of his mother, Mary. The worshipper meditates on each of the events or *'mysteries of the faith'* for as long as it takes to say the *'Our Father'* once and the *'Hail Mary'* ten times.

After meditating on each mystery, the worshipper says: *'Glory to the Father'* before going on to the next mystery.

The *'Our Father'* can be found under the heading: *The Lord's Prayer* on page 33.

The *'Hail Mary'* is this prayer:
'Hail Mary, full of grace, the Lord is with thee
Blessed art thou among women, and blessed is the fruit of thy womb, Jesus Christ.
Holy Mary, Mother of God; pray for us sinners now and in the hour of our death.'

The events or mysteries are divided into three groups:
the joyful mysteries:
  the annunciation
  visitation
  nativity
  presentation in the Temple
  finding in the Temple.
the sorrowful mysteries:
  the agony in the garden
  scourging
  crown of thorns
  carrying of the cross
  crucifixion
the glorious mysteries:
  the resurrection
  ascension
  descent of the Holy Spirit
  assumption of the Virgin
  coronation of the Virgin

All the mysteries, except the last two, refer to Bible incidents which will be explored in Chapters 4 and 5. The last two mysteries, according to Roman Catholic belief, flow from all that is written about Mary in the Gospel.

In addition to the Rosary, there is a rich variety of prayers for private worship, many of them centuries old. Here are two of the classic prayers of Christianity which come from the Roman Catholic tradition:

Prayer of St Francis of Assisi
'Lord, make me an instrument of your peace.
Where there is hatred, let me bring love;
Where there is injury, pardon;
Where there is doubt, faith;
Where there is despair, hope;
Where there is darkness; light;
Where there is sadness, let me bring joy'.

Prayer of St Richard of Chichester

'Thank you, Lord Jesus,
for all the benefits which you have given me,
for all the pains and insults which you have borne for me.
O most merciful Redeemer, friend and brother,
may I know you more clearly,
love you more dearly,
and follow you more nearly.   AMEN.'

If you think these words are vaguely familiar you may realize that the last words of the prayer form the basis of the song 'Day by Day' from the musical *Godspell*.

Church of Scotland

Private worship among members of the Church of Scotland usually takes the form of Bible study and personal prayers. There are many books of Bible readings and prayers to guide them and their prayers may be suggested by what they read as well as by their special needs. Here are some suggestions for prayer given by one of these guides. The Themes for Intercession and for Thanksgiving express the interest and concern which Christians share for the whole of life.

Themes for Intercession

Our own nation; all nations; the peace of the world.
Our neighbours, friends and relations.
Minority groups; those of other races, cultures and faiths.
Artists and dancers, writers, musicians and poets.

Themes for Thanksgiving

The communities whose life we share.
The power of Christ to transform suffering.
Truth we have learned; discoveries that mankind has made.
Christ's victory over sin, sickness and death.

A Day Prayer

Eternal God and Father, you create us
by your power and redeem us by your love:
guide and strengthen us by your Spirit,
that we may give ourselves in love and service
to one another and to you; through Jesus Christ
our Lord. AMEN.'

A Night Prayer

Lighten our darkness, Lord, we pray;
and in your mercy defend us from all
perils and dangers of this night;
for the love of your only Son, our
Saviour Jesus Christ. AMEN.

TEST YOUR UNDERSTANDING

● What a person prays for, both for himself and for others, can give us a clue to the kind of person he is. Study carefully each of the prayers and the list of Themes for Intercession. Build up a table as follows:

CHRISTIAN PRAYER	
Things asked for oneself (PETITIONS)	Things asked for others (INTERCESSIONS)

MAKING A NEW WORLD: PART 1

4

□□

The main ideas and beliefs which lie behind Christian worship can be traced to the Bible, and in particular to the first four books of the New Testament. These books announce the Gospel, or Good News, that God's kingdom has begun. The Gospel writers present the life of Jesus as evidence of this. We look in this chapter at stories from Luke's Gospel which show us what Christians believe about God's kingdom.

Who was Luke?

Unlike most of the other writers of the New Testament he was a Greek, not a Jew, though he shows that he is very familiar with the Jewish scriptures and the Jewish way of life. He was a friend of Paul, the greatest of the early Christian missionaries, and travelled with him on several of his journeys, including his long adventurous journey by land and sea to Rome. In fact tradition suggests that Luke was Paul's only companion during the last days of his imprisonment in Rome before Paul was executed.

Paul calls him 'Our dear doctor' and there is a particular emphasis in Luke's Gospel on stories about Jesus healing people.

Luke was the author not only of one of the Gospels, but also of The Acts of the Apostles. His Gospel shows God at work through Jesus in bringing about a new world. The Acts of the Apostles shows God at work through the early Christians in continuing the work of building this new world. Chapter 7 of *Search* looks at Christians today and considers whether or not the work of building a new world is continuing. Some of the events in the Acts of the Apostles seem to be based on Luke's own eyewitness accounts, other parts were probably based on the memories of Paul. Luke, however, did not witness any of the events which he wrote about in his Gospel. Bible scholars believe that Luke used three different sources of information for his Gospel stories –

Mark's Gospel which it is believed was written about A.D. 65,

a collection of the sayings of Jesus which the writer of Matthew's Gospel also used,

a source or sources which only Luke had access to.

It is thought that Luke wrote his Gospel sometime between A.D. 75 and 85.

Luke is symbolized by the winged ox

What Kind of Book Is a Gospel?

A gospel is not a biography of Jesus. Many of the facts which a biography would deal with are omitted altogether from the gospels. Although the Gospel stories are about real people and real events, they are first and foremost religious stories with meaning, told to build and develop the faith of their readers. So it is important that, as we read them, we ask such questions as these:

Why did Luke choose this story?

How does this story illustrate the claim that God's kingdom had begun?

What ideas about God's kingdom does this story teach?

God's Kingdom

As we have seen, the main concern of the Gospel writers was to announce that God's kingdom had begun. The popular picture of the kingdom among the Jews of Jesus' time was of a prosperous way of life in their own land. Their ideal was to live in peace and safety for ever, free from their enemies and with plenty to eat and drink: 'secure in a land full of corn and wine'.

Jesus' picture of God's kingdom, as presented to us by Luke, was quite different from the popular picture. Luke, more than any other of the Gospel writers, stresses that God's kingdom is for all people. When we come to Luke's stories, look out for references to Gentiles (non-Jews), Samaritans (people related to the Jews but looked down upon by them), the poor, the outcast, women (who held an inferior position in Jewish society at the time of Jesus) as well as to the 'respectable' members of Jewish society.

But how are members of the kingdom to behave? Luke says 'as children of God'. And as a guide to how a child of God should behave he points to Jesus as the perfect son of God.

Prayer, repentance and forgiveness are themes central to Luke's teaching about God's kingdom and we will explore what Luke has to say about them and discuss their relevance, if any, to 20th century living.

We began this chapter by referring to the connection between the Bible and worship. Two sets of stories made such an impact on the early Church that they formed the basis for the two great festivals of the Christian Year, Christmas and Easter. We will therefore explore these stories in the following chapter on the Christian Calendar, and begin Luke's account of the Good News with his story of the baptism of Jesus.

The Son of God: King and Servant

The stories of the baptism and temptations of Jesus reveal the struggle which Jesus went through in working out how he should undertake the work to which he felt called. The language of the stories belongs to the history and ancient traditions of the Jewish people. Phrases such as 'heaven was opened', 'the Holy Spirit came down' and 'a voice came from heaven' would have immediately reminded readers of stories from the Jewish scriptures. The ideas which they introduce, however, relate to issues which are the concern of each generation, the four key questions which *Search* explores.

The Baptism of Jesus   *Luke 3:3, 21-22*
John the Baptist is introduced as working in the plain of the River Jordan, the largest and most famous river of Palestine. His teaching was stern and clear:

'Turn away from your sins and be baptized and God will forgive your sins.'

This sculpture from a church in Moissac, S. France, shows a vision of Jesus as King. How does this compare with the Jesus of the temptations?

The famous Jewish historian, Josephus, had this to say about John:

> 'He was a good man and commanded the Jews to practise virtue by exercising justice towards one another and devotion towards God, and to come together to baptism.'

It is probable that baptism was already in use among the Jews as part of the ceremony by which a Gentile who wished to become a Jew was symbolically washed of his sins. John preaches that even the Jews themselves had to change their ways and ask for God's forgiveness as a preparation for entering his kingdom.

The experience which Luke describes occurred while Jesus was praying. The words of the 'voice' indicate what was going on in Jesus' mind. They come from two songs from the Jewish scriptures, songs which would have been familiar to all Jewish boys. The phrase 'You are my own dear Son' is an echo of Psalm 2, which formed part of the ancient coronation ceremonies of the Jewish kings. The psalm later came to be associated with the Messiah, the great leader which Jews believed God would send to rescue them from their suffering.

The second part of the 'voice', 'I am pleased with you' comes from a song about God's Servant, who has been chosen to carry true religion to the whole world, and who will suffer and die in carrying out his work.

Taken together, the words suggest Jesus realizing that he was the long awaited Messiah, but not one who would bring about God's kingdom through might and power, but through patience and service.

41

'Solitaire' from
Miserere by
Georges Roualt

The Temptations of Jesus   Luke 4: 1–13

Time and time again Luke makes clear that when people met Jesus they were
made to feel that God himself was present. Describing Jesus as being 'full of the
Holy Spirit' is one way of saying this. All the qualities that people associated with
God were to be found in Jesus.

Today we usually think of temptation happening in the mind, and so it does.
The story of Jesus' temptations, using the language and ideas familiar to 1st
century readers, pictures Jesus being confronted by a real, visible Devil. The
scene is the desert, where Jesus has fasted for a long time. Is the Messiah really
to follow the way of the servant? Surely there are quicker and surer ways of
bringing about God's kingdom?

The first temptation is: *'If you are God's Son, order this stone to turn to
bread.'* Jesus was hungry after his fasting, and knew that many of his fellow
countrymen were never far from starvation. There would be no shortage of
followers for a Messiah who offered food to the hungry. In fact one of the most
popular pictures of God's kingdom was of a great feast. It is good to feed the
hungry and Christians today join with others of goodwill in caring for those in
need. But people need more than food and drink for their bodies. Their minds
and spirits have to be fed as well or they will not become fully developed human
beings. The way in which the Bible says this is: *'Man cannot live by bread alone.'*

Jesus then sees in his mind all the countries of the world. *'All this could be
yours,'* the Devil says, *'if you worship me.'* This is the temptation to take the
traditional path of the conqueror. Be a greater king than David, mightier than

Caesar himself. This was certainly the Messiah that most of the Jews longed for. Many passages in the Jewish scriptures seemed to point to a king who would take up the sword. The very Psalm that had been in Jesus' mind at his baptism says:

> *'Ask, and I will give you all the nations;*
> *the whole earth will be yours.*
> *You will break them with an iron rod;*
> *You will shatter them in pieces like a clay pot.'* (Psalm 2: 8–9)

But was the war-path truly the way of God the Father?

Jesus answered: *'Worship the Lord your God and serve him only.'* Serving God rules out the path of violence as the way of spreading his kingdom.

This second temptation followed Jesus through all his work in Galilee and to the very end in Jerusalem. Amongst his followers were Zealots, a group of Jews who wished to rise up against the Romans and drive them out of their land. The crowds of Galilee tried to seize him by force and compel him to become their king. Even in the garden of Gethsemane his eager disciples wanted to use their swords.

In the third temptation Jesus imagines himself perched on the highest point of the Temple, a sheer drop of 450 feet to the valley below. The Devil says *'If you are God's Son, throw yourself down from here.'* Scripture says: 'God will order his angels to take good care of you'. (Psalm 91:11) Surely if Jesus descended miraculously from the Temple pinnacle into the sacred courts everyone would believe that God had sent him? Certainly the Jewish people always thought of God as doing wondrous things.

Jesus remembered the story of the Hebrews in the desert when they demanded a sign that God was with them. They were told not to put God to the test. To say 'Prove to me that you love me.' is another way of saying 'I do not trust you'. Jesus refuses to follow the way of signs and wonders. The way of magic is not the way of the kingdom. The last verse of the story of the temptations says: *'When the Devil finished tempting Jesus in every way, he left him for a while.'* All the temptations were to occur again and again in Jesus' mind as he tried to fulfil his work as the Messiah. Even at the cross passers-by jeered at him: *'He saved others; let him save himself if he is the Messiah whom God has chosen!'*

The experiences which the stories of the baptism and temptations describe were probably told by Jesus to his disciples in the weeks and months before his crucifixion to help them appreciate the way he had come and they themselves were to follow.

TEST YOUR UNDERSTANDING

● *'Exercise justice towards one another and devotion towards God.'*
Rewrite John's message in your own words.
● Why would John's message that the Jews had to 'turn away from their sins and be baptized' shock some of his listeners?
● Prepare two columns, one headed 'Messiah' and the other 'God's Servant'. Write three words or phrases in each column to describe the different qualities associated with each title.
● Why do you think both titles were used to describe Jesus?
● Describe in your own words the three ideas which came to Jesus in the wilderness, and explain why he rejected each of them.

God's Kingdom in Words

Christians believe that members of God's kingdom are called to be 'children of God', in other words, to share God's qualities, and so we begin with the story which best sums up Jesus' teaching about God. The story is usually known as the Prodigal Son or the Lost Son, but could more appropriately be called the Loving Father.

The Lost Son   Luke 15: 11-32
This has been called the most famous short story in the world. The younger son of a well-to-do man demanded his share of his father's property. So the father gave both the sons their proper share. The younger boy sold what he had and left home at once with the cash in his pocket. He went far away and soon spent every penny of his money.

Then a famine sprang up and he had no work and nothing to eat. He was glad enough to find a job looking after pigs – the filthiest work a Jew could think of. He was so hungry that he would have been glad to eat the bean pods that were the pigs' food. Then he came to his senses and his mind was filled with thoughts of home. 'Even my father's hired helpers have more than they can eat, while I perish here. I will go back to my father and say I'm sorry.' So he got up and headed for home.

The father had never forgotten his lost son. He saw him coming a long way off and ran and threw his arms around him and kissed him. The boy began his apology, but the father interrupted him, shouting to his servants to bring clothes and a ring for the boy's finger and shoes for his feet. He was to be his loved son again, not a slave. 'Let's have a party!' cried the father.

It is his father who takes the lead in the story. Jesus is telling his hearers, outcasts and Pharisees alike, how God the Father rejoices in finding one of his lost sons, no matter what the world thinks of them or what they might think of themselves.

The parable does not end there. There were two sons. The older boy was lost to his father, too, though he had stayed at home and worked hard. He was just as self-centred as his younger brother. His favourite words were 'I, me, my, mine.' He was so wrapped up in himself and his rights that he could not

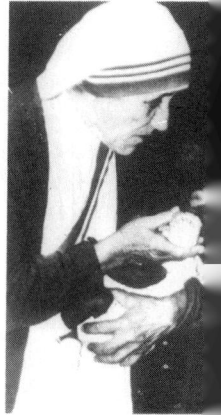

Mother Teresa with one of her orphans

understand his father's joy when the prodigal came home. He thinks the worst of what he has been up to in the faraway land. He would not even acknowledge his brother. 'This son of yours,' he called him.

The father went to both boys. This time he begged his older son to come in. 'We must have a party,' he said. 'Your brother is alive and found again.'

Jesus told the parable so that his hearers could make up their own minds. They had to decide for themselves, outcast and righteous alike, 'Is this what God is like?'

Christians, as we have seen, are called to be sons of God, they are to share his qualities. If God acts like the loving father in the parable, so must the members of his kingdom as the following story makes clear.

The Parable of the Good Samaritan   Luke 10: 25-37

The parable of the Good Samaritan has become one of the best-known and best-loved of Jesus' stories. It would be quite different with his first hearers. They would find it quite startling and revolutionary. None of them would expect a Samaritan – a hated and despised foreigner – to be the hero of a story told by a Jew.

Jesus was challenged by a teacher of the Law to answer: 'What must I do to receive eternal life?' This is another way of saying: 'What have I to do to be a member of God's kingdom?' Jesus invited the man to answer for himself, from his knowledge of the Law. The Rabbi gave the traditional answer, the great commandment which every Jew knew off by heart from earliest childhood: *'Love the Lord your God with all your heart, with all your soul, with all your strength and with all your mind.'* (Deuteronomy 6:5) He added another familiar Jewish rule: *'Love your neighbour as yourself.'* (Leviticus 19:18)

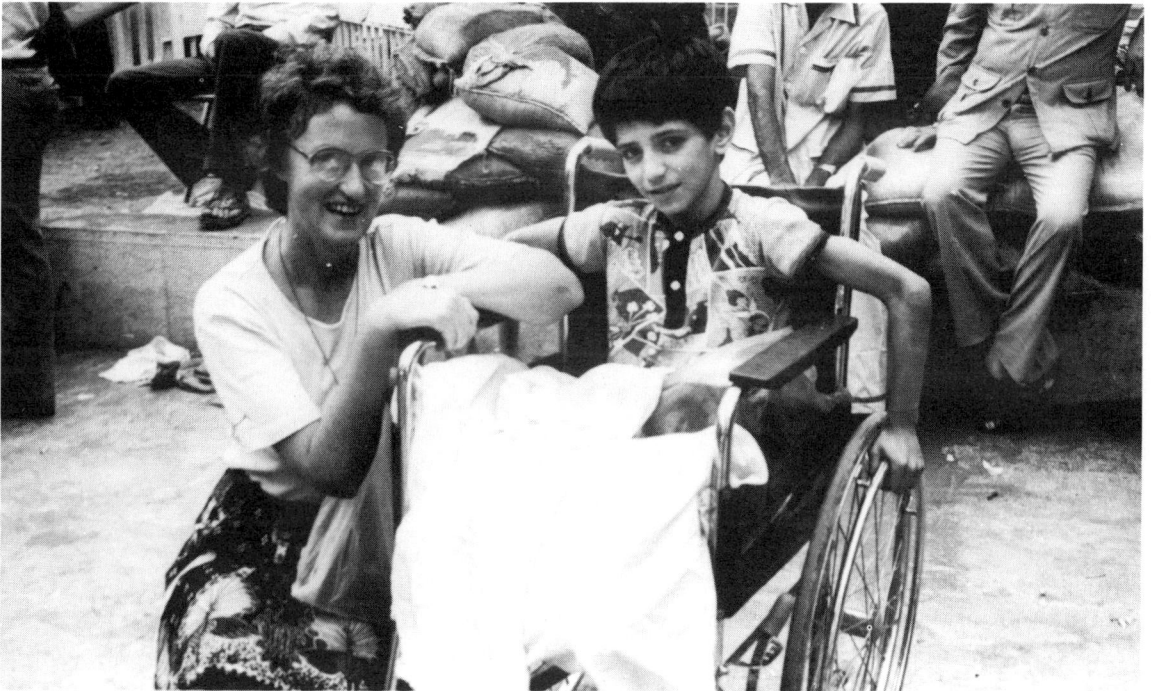

Sister Joy Riordan, one of the helpers sent to Lebanon by Christian Aid

Jesus said: 'You are right!' No Jew could give a better answer. But the teacher of the Law wanted to catch Jesus out. 'Who is my neighbour?' He believed the answer was quite clear in the Law: 'the son of your own people'. One's neighbour was any fellow-Jew, but no one else.

It is at this point that Jesus tells his story. A man going down the rocky desert road from Jerusalem to Jericho was attacked by robbers. They robbed him of everything, beat him up, and left him by the roadside stripped and half-dead.

A priest came down the road. Did he know the Law about 'Love your neighbour'? Certainly he did! As a good Jew he knew every word of the Law. But a man lying by the roadside might be dead. Jews believed that if they came into contact with a corpse they became unclean in the eyes of God and could not perform their religious duties until they had cleansed themselves through rituals laid down in the Law. Because there were so many priests, they seldom had the opportunity to serve in the Temple. If the man by the side of the road was dead, the priest would miss his turn at the Temple. So he did not go near. He walked past on the other side. Then a Levite, a Temple servant, came by. He looked at the man, but walked by on the other side, for much the same reason as the priest.

A Samaritan came along, a foreigner and a natural enemy of the Jew. He does not pause to ask himself: 'Who is my neighbour?' All his actions are full of concern for the wounded man. He pours oil and wine on the man's wounds. The wine would clean the wound, and the oil soothe the pain. Then he bandages him, puts him on his own animal and takes him to an inn.

The Samaritan's concern does not end with shelter for the night. An Eastern inn was merely a roof over travellers' heads and a shelter for their animals. 'He took care of him' implied food, drink, bedding, care of his wounds, watching over him all night long. Next morning he gives the innkeeper two silver coins with the promise of more if required, and the instruction: 'Take care of him.' Only then does he go on his way. Jesus ended his story by asking: 'In your opinion, which of the three acted as neighbour to the man attacked by robbers?' The teacher of the Law could not bring himself to use the name 'Samaritan', but he gave the right answer: 'the one who was kind to him'. Then Jesus said: 'You go, then, and do the same!' To be a neighbour is much more than memorising rules and regulations. It is caring in action, for everyone who is in need.

Jesus taught at times through stories, and at other times he used straightforward teaching to make his message clear. For those who manage to miss the point of the two parables, the message is repeated clearly in the following sayings.

Love Your Enemies   Luke 6: 27–36

The Law of the Jewish Scriptures was clear and plain: *'Love your neighbour as you love yourself, I am the Lord.'* (Leviticus 19:18) All good Jews had it off by heart. The Jews, however, as we have seen, were equally clear about its meaning. The Law referred only to one's fellow Jews. They were 'your neighbour'. All others were Gentiles, foreigners, enemies. Jesus made a unique and extraordinary demand: *'Love your enemies'*. He also made very clear who he meant: *'those who hate you . . . who curse you . . . who ill-treat you.'*

In English the word 'love' is used for a wide range of feelings and behaviour. The Greek language in which the New Testament was written has three different words for love. When Jesus says 'Love your enemies', he does not mean 'Fall in

EL DIALOGO POR LA PAZ,
UNA URGENCIA PARA NUESTRO TIEMPO

Joannes Paulus PP II
Juan Pablo II

XVI Jornada Mundial de la Paz

A poster issued by the Bishops of El Salvador calling on people to love their enemy. Look for the symbols of peace.

love with them', nor does he mean that Christians should have the same feelings for their enemies as they have for their family and friends. What he does mean is that the Christian should have a determined and active concern for the good of others, no matter who they are. And Jesus is talking to people who live in an occupied country and whose everyday life is filled with constant reminders of their enemies' presence.

Most rules begin with the words: 'Do not . . .' Jesus' command is both positive and revolutionary, probably the most revolutionary of all his teaching. Generosity of spirit is to be the distinguishing feature of the follower of Jesus. There are to be no exceptions to the rule of caring for others. In this way, the follower of Jesus will become a son of God, who cares for all, good and bad alike.

TEST YOUR UNDERSTANDING

● Make up three sentences which show clearly the different meanings of 'love.'
● As a class, debate the motion: 'Jesus' teaching about loving enemies is nonsense.'
● Jesus said that God 'was good to the ungrateful and wicked'. Some people think that this is not fair. What do you think?
● Describe in your own words what it means to become 'sons of . . . God'.
● Why did Jesus tell the teacher of the Law a story instead of giving him a straight answer?
● In groups write out your own modern version of the story of the Good Samaritan. Act it out in front of the class and be prepared to defend both the plot of the story and the characters chosen.

For those who may be undecided, Jesus gives a warning about the cost of being a member of the kingdom.

The Cost of Being a Disciple   Luke 14: 25–33

In his own district of Galilee Jesus attracted enthusiastic crowds. They flocked to listen to him and to wonder at his works of healing. They were natural rebels against the hated Roman power, and no doubt many Galileans hoped that Jesus would lead them against their enemies. Even among the closest disciples he had members of the patriotic anti-Roman Zealot party.

In this passage Jesus makes it very plain to the crowds that following him will not mean victory and glory. It will mean suffering and a cross. They all knew what the cruel Roman punishment of crucifixion meant. Anyone following Jesus must turn away even from his nearest and dearest – father, mother, wife, children, brothers and sisters. A disciple must be as loyal as a soldier enlisting in the army. Jesus tells two parables to underline what he means.

A man planning to build a tower on his farm will sit down first and work out what it will cost, to make sure that he has enough money to finish the job. If he can only lay the foundation and build no more, everyone will laugh at him.

If a king goes out with ten thousand men to fight another king whose army is twenty thousand strong, he will sit down first and decide if he is strong enough to do battle. If he isn't, he will send messengers to meet the other king and ask for terms of peace while he is still a long way off.

So, said Jesus, none of you can be my disciple unless he gives up everything he has. If you have to plan carefully to build a tower or to fight a battle, you have to think out just as clearly what it means to be my disciple. Weigh up the worth, and be ready to pay the price.

How did Jesus gain the strength to follow the way of the cross? At each crisis in his life he is presented as praying to God for guidance. Jesus was known as a man of prayer. It is natural that his disciples who wished to follow in his footsteps should say to him, 'Lord, teach us to pray.' Jesus' reply gives his disciples a model prayer which has been used by all Christians everywhere from that day to this.

Jesus' Teaching on Prayer   Luke 11: 1–4

Luke's version of the Lord's prayer is brief and basic. The version which forms part of most acts of public worship can be found on page 33.

'Father:'
The word which Jesus uses for 'Father' is the word which a child would use speaking to his dad. Though, as we have seen, the title 'Son of God' was an ancient one in Jewish tradition, Jesus gives it a new meaning. Son of God is no longer merely another title for the Messiah. It describes a person who knows God so well he can call him 'Dad'.

'May your holy name be honoured:
may your kingdom come.'
For a Jew a person's name meant not only what he was called but what he was like, his character or nature. Jesus is asking that God's holiness and love be displayed throughout the world, in other words that God's kingdom would grow.

A Canadian poster calls for people to become priests

'Give us day by day the food we need.'
A reminder to the Christian that he depends on God for the basic needs of life.

'Forgive us our sins, for we forgive everyone who does us wrong.'
A reminder of the need for forgiveness. People cannot expect to be forgiven by God if they do not forgive other people. Note the connection between this petition or request and Jesus' teaching on loving enemies.

'And do not bring us to hard testing.'
A reminder that the members of the early Church who first repeated this prayer faced the 'test' of suffering and persecution and martyrdom. Christians have been tested in different ways throughout the centuries since then. At times their lives have been in danger; often it is their integrity or honesty which is at risk, rather than their lives or freedom. 'Testing' takes many forms.

Many of those who heard Jesus teach would regard a world in which people put his teaching into practice as a dream world. The following stories give Jesus' reply.

The parable of the Mustard Seed Luke 13: 18–19
The parable of the Yeast Luke 13: 20–21

Each of these short stories stresses the contrast between a very small beginning and a great ending. The tiny mustard seed grew to be a tree, big enough to let the birds make their nests in its branches. A housewife takes a very little yeast, only a few crumbs, and mixes it with forty litres of flour.

Both stories are used by Jesus as pictures of the growth of God's kingdom from very small beginnings.

_____TEST YOUR UNDERSTANDING_____

- Explain the new meaning which Jesus gives to the old title 'Son of God.'
- Rewrite the Lord's Prayer in your own words.

God's Kingdom in Action

Just as Jesus' teaching is concerned with God's kingdom, so his actions are presented by Luke as showing that God's kingdom has arrived. Luke's stories focus on the theme of health and wholeness to show what life in the kingdom is like. Jesus restores to health and wholeness those who are suffering from mental and physical illnesses or handicaps and also those who are cut off from the rest of society for whatever reason.

A Man with an Evil Spirit   Luke 4: 31–37

Capernaum was a town on the northern shore of the Sea of Galilee. It was a busy and prosperous fishing port with a Roman military garrison on the hill overlooking everyone. Jesus made his home there with Simon Peter and the other fishermen disciples and Capernaum became the centre of his teaching and healing in Galilee.

It was the custom in the Jewish synagogue to invite a well-known Rabbi or teacher to read the scriptures on the Sabbath and to speak about them to the congregation. The people of Capernaum were all amazed at Jesus' way of speaking. His words were powerful and rang true. He spoke as if he knew God.

Suddenly he was interrupted by the screams of a man who was out of his mind. Any disease or illness which involved loss of control was described in the ancient world as demon possession. The loss of control suggested the presence of an invading power. It was only through a greater power that a person could be freed from the demons.

The man screamed out: 'What do you want with us? I know who you are; you are God's holy messenger!' Jesus ordered the evil spirit: *'Be quiet and come out of the man!'* Once again Luke comments on Jesus' authority, not merely in what he says but in what he does. Through his action, Jesus is not just showing compassion for the man by healing him, but is showing that God's power is at work freeing people from the power of evil; in other words God's kingdom has arrived.

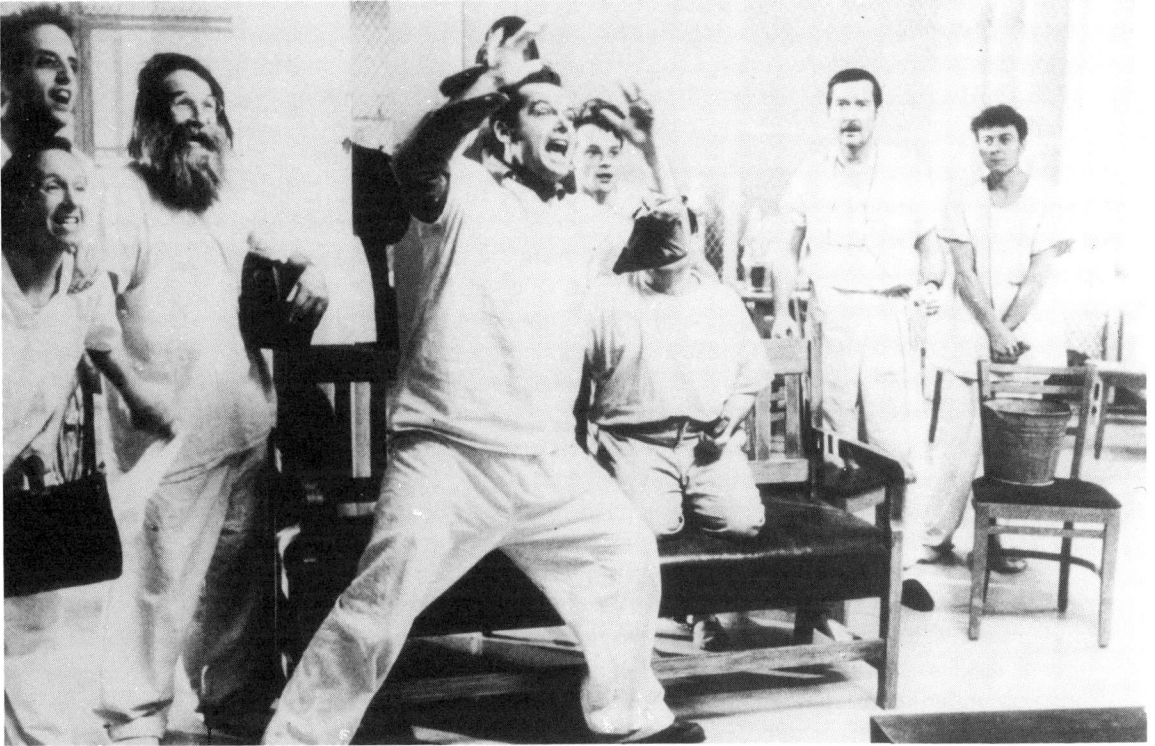

Jesus Heals Many People   Luke 4: 38–41

When Jesus left the synagogue in Capernaum he went to Simon Peter's house. Simon's mother-in-law was sick with a high fever. Note Luke, the doctor, paying attention to medical detail. They asked Jesus to help. He stood at her bedside and ordered the fever to leave her just as he had earlier ordered the evil spirit to leave the man in the synagogue. At once the fever left her and she got up and went about her household duties, ready to attend to her guests.

These two acts of healing took place on the Sabbath day. No doubt Jesus was eventually blamed by the religious leaders for 'working' on the Sabbath. Jewish law was very strict about this. The Sabbath begins at sunset on Friday and lasts until sunset on Saturday. The people waited until after sunset before bringing their friends and relatives to Jesus. Luke tells us that Jesus went from one to another and put his hands on them one by one and healed them all. Readers of Luke's Gospel would be reminded of the words of Isaiah the prophet.

'The blind will be able to see,
and the deaf will hear.
The lame will leap and dance,
and those who cannot speak will shout for joy.'

Jesus Preaches in the Synagogue   Luke 4: 42–44

At daybreak, after a long night of healing, Jesus left Capernaum and went off to a lonely place to pray. But the crowds started looking for him and tracked him down. Naturally, they wanted to keep him in Capernaum. But Jesus said: *'God sent me to preach about His Kingdom in other towns also.'* So he taught in synagogues all through the country.

Jesus Heals a Roman Officer's Servant   *Luke 7: 1–10*

Luke never forgets that he is writing to commend the story of Jesus to Gentiles in the Roman world. Here he tells how Jesus helped a Gentile, a Roman centurion. A centurion was a soldier in charge of a hundred men. It was a very important post in the Roman army.

Once again the incident takes place in Capernaum. The centurion had a slave he was very fond of, who was sick and at the point of death. The centurion had heard about Jesus as he was bound to do from the gossip of Capernaum. He did not come himself, perhaps thinking that a Jewish holy man would not speak to a Roman. But he had enough influence among some of the leading Jews of the place to send them to Jesus, begging him to come and heal his slave. He might be a heathen foreigner in their eyes, and a soldier at that, but they spoke very strongly on behalf of the centurion. 'This man really deserves your help. He loves our people and it was he who built a synagogue for us.' This was a very warm and unusual tribute indeed.

Jesus went with them, but on the way the centurion sent friends to say: 'I do not deserve to have you come into my house, nor am I worthy to come to you myself. Just give the order, and my slave will get well!' He was aware that a good Jew would not readily enter the house of a Gentile. He did not want to embarrass this Jewish healer. He did, however, know all about authority. He himself was a soldier under the command of his superior officers, and in turn he had men under his orders. He knew that his every word was obeyed by his men and by his slave. 'Go!' meant 'Go!' and 'Come!' meant 'Come' and 'Do this!' meant 'Do this!'

Jesus was amazed at the message from the centurion. He turned round and spoke to the crowd following him: *'I tell you, I have never found faith like this, not even among our own Jewish people.'*

Luke notes that this was the highest praise Jesus ever spoke, and it was said about a Gentile, a foreigner. And when the messengers went back to the Roman barracks, they found the slave well and strong again.

Healing a Blind Beggar   *Luke 18: 35–43*

Jericho was a busy town in the Jordan Valley, near where the River Jordan flows into the Dead Sea. It was known as the city of 'palms', a prosperous, sunny place with fine buildings and gardens and orchards. The fruit and balm, a sweet smelling ointment, of Jericho were exported to every part of the Roman Empire. Jesus and his disciples came that way on the road to Jerusalem along with crowds of other Jewish pilgrims. By the roadside there was a blind man, begging. When the blind man heard the noise of the crowd going by, he asked: 'What is this?' Someone told him: 'Jesus of Nazareth is passing by.'

Instantly the beggar began shouting out to draw attention to himself. But he did not call out: 'Jesus of Nazareth!' Instead, his cry was: *'Jesus! Son of David! Take pity on me!'* The beggar could not see Jesus, but he must have heard of him. He relied entirely on the quickness of his ears. He must have heard the popular talk of the crowd that this teacher was perhaps the one who was to lead them against their enemies and be a kingly Messiah of David's line. The people in the crowd told the beggar to shut up. The words 'Son of David' were dangerous. The Roman authorities were always on the look-out for treason and rebellion.

The Church continues to care today as in this gift of an ambulance for the sick of Nigeria.

Jesus stopped and told them to bring the blind man to him. When he stood in front of him, Jesus said: *'What do you want me to do for you?'* The beggar's reply was quite clear: *'Lord, I want to see again!'* He hadn't always been blind and reduced to the dust of the roadside. He wanted his sight more than anything in the world. Jesus was equally direct: *'Then see! Your faith has made you well!'* At once the man was able to see and he joined the crowd about Jesus, calling out his praise to God. Luke is again reminding us of Isaiah's words. In the day that God comes among them:
'The blind will be able to see' (Isaiah 35: 5)

Jesus and Zacchaeus *Luke 19: 1–10*
Jesus came through Jericho and his next encounter was with a man called Zacchaeus who was a chief tax-collector and very rich. Luke says a lot here in a short phrase. The name 'Zacchaeus' means 'pure' but no citizen of Jericho would have thought of him in that way. His work as a tax-collector employed by the hated Romans made him an outcast and unclean to his fellow-Jews. The citizens of Jericho hated Zacchaeus for the daily work he did and the fact that he grew rich on it.

Zacchaeus was very anxious to see Jesus, but he was a little man and he could not see over the heads of the crowds. In any case, the people were hostile, and he knew it, and they certainly would not make way for him. So he ran on ahead and climbed up a tree to watch as Jesus came along the road.

When Jesus came to the place he stopped and looked up and spoke directly to Zacchaeus. *'Hurry down, Zacchaeus, because I must stay in your home today!'* The effect on Zacchaeus was instant and extraordinary. He tumbled out of the tree and began to pour out a welcome. The crowd took it very badly. 'This man,' they raged at Jesus, 'is going to be guest in the house of a sinner!' It was bad enough that Jesus even spoke to a man like Zacchaeus. Now he was going to do what no decent Jew in the place would ever do – go to his house and eat there.

Zacchaeus knew the hatred and hostility of the crowd. He deserved it, but Jesus did not. Instantly he poured out his guilt and a promise. He raised his voice

53

so that everyone could hear. *'Listen, Lord, I will give half of everything I have to the poor, and if I have cheated anyone, I will pay him back four times as much.'* He has had a complete change of heart and broken with his shameful past. Zacchaeus went far beyond what even the Jewish Law required. The Law laid down the rules for repayment for wrongs done:

'When anyone is unfaithful to the Lord and commits a wrong against someone, he must confess his sin and make full repayment, plus an additional twenty per cent, to the person he has wronged.' (Numbers 5: 5–7)

Jesus said: *'Today healing has come to this house. This man also is a son of Abraham.'* He restores Zacchaeus to the dignity of his place in God's kingdom as one of God's people.

It is only Luke who tells us this story. He sees Jesus as one who seeks out and invites lost men and women into God's kingdom.

TEST YOUR UNDERSTANDING

● Read the following verse which comes from a poem by the prophet Isaiah about what life will be like when God's kingdom comes:

'The blind will be able to see,
and the deaf to hear.
The lame will leap and dance,
and those who cannot speak will
shout for joy.'
(Isaiah 35: 5–6)

Write a short report in your own words about an incident in which Jesus cured a person who suffered from a physical illness or handicap. How does the above verse help us to understand why Luke includes such stories in his Gospel?
● Write a short report in your own words about an incident in which Jesus cured a person who suffered from mental illness. Why did Luke include such stories in his Gospel?
● Which healing stories are used to illustrate the following:
    love your enemies,
    God's care for the sinner?
● What are the ten most important requirements for a healthy life?
● What evidence is there of the Church today continuing Jesus' work of making people healthy?

The Passion Story

The final part of Luke's Gospel is usually known as the Passion Story – passion meaning suffering. It describes in some detail the events which led to the death of Jesus on the cross, as well as the story of the Resurrection. Luke has to explain to his Gentile readers how this popular teacher and healer came to be put to death as a criminal. The Passion Story was continually recited in the early Church and it set the pattern for worship in Holy Week and Easter, the most important days in the calendar of the Church.

The Plot against Jesus   *Luke 22: 1–2*
In this brief introduction Luke puts the blame for the death of Jesus firmly on 'the chief priests and teachers of the Law', in other words, the religious leaders of the Jews. They wanted to act secretly because they were afraid of the people. They dared not arrest Jesus openly during the days of the Passover Festival, because it might bring about a riot. All through the events of Jesus' last week Luke is anxious to make clear to his Gentile readers that the Jews rather than the Roman authorities were responsible for Jesus' death.

The annual Passover Festival lasted seven days and was the most important time of the Jewish year. It continues to this day, and commemorates the time long ago when God delivered the Jews from slavery in Egypt. Luke notes that in his day the festival was sometimes called the 'feast of unleavened bread' because for seven days on end unleavened bread was eaten.

At the time of Jesus the central feature of the Passover was the sacrifice of a lamb at the Temple in Jerusalem. The pilgrims then took their lambs to their homes or inns and ate them with bitter herbs and unleavened bread in their family groups.

Judas Agrees to Betray Jesus   *Luke 22: 3–6*
We know nothing about Judas Iscariot except that he betrayed Jesus, and that keeps his name alive all through history. He was apparently one of the twelve disciples. He went secretly to the chief priests at a suitable moment, away from the crowds, about how he could betray Jesus to them. They were very pleased to hear this, and offered to pay him for his treachery.

There have been endless arguments about why Judas wanted to betray Jesus. Luke says simply that Satan entered into him. In other words, this is part of the continuing story of the battle between God and Satan which came to a climax with the death and resurrection of Jesus.

Jesus Prepares to Eat the Passover Meal   *Luke 22: 7–13*
It would appear that Jesus made careful preparations so that he and his disciples were not disturbed at the Passover meal. He sent Peter and John, his two most trusted disciples, to go and prepare the meal. Naturally they asked: *'Where do you want us to get it ready?'* Jesus gave them strange but clear instructions. *'As you go into the city you will see a man carrying a jar of water. Follow him to the house that he enters and say to the owner: "The Teacher says, Where is the room where my disciples and I will eat the Passover?"'. He will show you a large furnished room upstairs, where you will get everything ready.'*

Peter and John went off and found everything just as Jesus said. Even in the crowded city a man carrying a jar of water would be an unusual sight, as that was normally woman's work. They followed him, came to the house, and were shown the upper room. It was furnished with tables and couches since it was the custom at the Passover meal to recline on a couch. No doubt Jesus had arranged with a friend in crowded Jerusalem that a room was to be at his disposal.

So the two men got everything ready. They would have to buy a lamb in the market-place and take it to the Temple to be sacrificed. Then they would prepare the meal according to age-old custom with the accompanying unleavened bread and bitter herbs and wine.

The Lord's Supper   Luke 22: 14–23

There are two different versions of Luke's story of the Last Supper to be found in the ancient documents on which the modern versions of the Bible are based. We will begin by looking at the details on which both agree.

Both versions state that the meal which Jesus celebrated with his disciples was a Passover meal. As we have seen, the Passover Festival commemorates the time long ago when God delivered the Jews from slavery in Egypt. Jesus gives new meaning to the meal by linking it with God's kingdom. As we saw in the story of the Temptations, a popular picture of the kingdom amongst the Jews at the time of Jesus was of a great feast. By linking the Passover meal with the great feast of the kingdom, Jesus is looking forward to the day when all people are delivered by God from slavery to 'the forces of evil.' The bread and wine mentioned in both versions of the story were two of the symbols used in the Passover meal. The versions differ when it comes to the words which Jesus associates with the bread and wine. The shorter version is as follows:

> Then Jesus took a cup, gave thanks to God, and said, 'Take this and share it among yourselves. I tell you that from now on I will not drink this wine until the Kingdom of God comes.
> Then he took a piece of bread, gave thanks to God, broke it, and gave it to them, saying, 'This is my body.'

The longer version adds:

> 'which is broken for you. Do this in memory of me.' In the same way, he gave the cup after the supper, saying. 'This cup is God's new covenant sealed with my blood, which is poured out for you.'

Most scholars believe that the shorter version was the original, and that the additional words were added to bring Luke's story into line with the accounts in Matthew and Mark and the earliest account of all, in the First Letter to the Corinthians. (I Corinthians 11: 23–25)

It is the longer version which is recited during the Liturgy of the Eucharist or Holy Communion which we studied in Chapter 3. The bread is the symbol of Jesus' broken body, and those who eat it share in the power of his life and the sacrifice of his death. The wine is the symbol of the shedding of his blood and the sign of a new covenant or agreement between God and his people. The old covenant, based on the Ten Commandments, was between God and the people of Israel and was written on tablets of stone. The new covenant, based on love, was between God and all people and would be written in people's hearts and consciences.

A minister leading the Communion Service

TEST YOUR UNDERSTANDING

● The bread and wine which Jesus shared with his disciples are full of meaning for Christians. Describe, in your own words, the ideas associated with the bread and wine.

● We have seen that one of the images used to describe God's kingdom was 'a great feast.' Why do you think a meal or feast is used as a symbol of God's kingdom?

Jesus Prays on the Mount of Olives   Luke 22: 39–46

It was the custom of Jesus and his disciples to leave Jerusalem at night. They probably had nowhere to stay in the over-crowded city which was packed from end to end with Passover pilgrims. They went across the valley of the River Kidron to the Mount of Olives, part of a range of hills to the east of Jerusalem.

There, in the quiet of the night, Jesus went apart from his friends to pray alone. His prayer was a cry of agony to God: *'Father, if you will, take this cup of suffering from me. Not my will, however, but your will be done.'* Jesus knew the horror and suffering he was to face. His prayer came from the depths of his spirit. When Jesus rose to his feet again, he found his disciples fast asleep, worn out by their distress. Luke pictures the great contrast between Jesus' agony of prayer and his sleeping disciples. But Jesus only says to them. *'Why are you sleeping? Get up and pray that you will not fall into temptation.'* If the horror of what was going to happen troubled him, then he knew that his followers would need all their strength to stand up to the darkness of events soon to fall on them.

57

The Arrest of Jesus   Luke 22: 47–53

A crowd of people arrived in the moonlight, led by Judas. At some point after the Last Supper he must have slipped away from the others to let the religious leaders know where they could find Jesus. Judas came up to Jesus and made to kiss him, the traditional sign of love and friendship. But Jesus rebuked him: *'Judas, would you betray the Son of Man with a kiss?'* When the other disciples saw what was going on they cried out: *'Shall we use our swords, Lord?'* They were armed and ready to fight to protect Jesus. Indeed, one of them was already in action. He struck the High Priest's slave and cut off his right ear. But Jesus said: *'Enough of this!'* He touched the man's ear and healed him.

Then he turned to the hostile crowd, the chief priests and officers of the temple guard and elders who had come to seize him. *'Did you come out with swords and clubs as though I was an outlaw?' I was with you openly in the temple every day and you did not try to arrest me. But now, when the forces of evil rule, this is your hour.'* This is yet another reference to the conflict between the forces of good and evil.

Jesus Is Brought before the Council   Luke 22:66–71

As soon as it was light the religious leaders of the Jews met together to deal with Jesus. These men formed the Council of the Jews known as the Sanhedrin. It was made up of seventy-one members, including priests, Pharisees and scribes, and the chairman was the High Priest. It was the Sanhedrin's business to administer the Jewish Law and to deal with those who broke it. They met in the Temple. The Sanhedrin had no power to pass the death sentence, but they were anxious to examine Jesus before they handed him over to the Roman civil authority for final trial and execution.

It was in no sense a proper legal trial. They had already made up their minds to find Jesus guilty and to destroy him. All they wanted at this point was to put together a good enough case to satisfy the Romans. They asked Jesus a leading question: *'Are you the Messiah?'* Jesus answered: *'You will not believe anything I say, and if I ask you a question you will not answer.'*

Then altogether they shouted: *'Are you, then, the Son of God?'* It was in their eyes, a blasphemous claim to make. Jesus merely answered: *'That is what you say.'*

It is impossible to know all that happened at this trial of Jesus before the Jewish religious leaders. The important fact is that they were determined to have him put to death. Jesus believed that God was with him, but there was no point in saying anything in the face of this enemy opposition. His kingdom, as he always taught, was not an earthly one.

Their verdict was: *'We don't need any witnesses. We have heard what he said.'* Their minds were made up, whether Jesus spoke or was silent before them.

Jesus Is Brought before Pilate   Luke 23: 1–5

Pontius Pilate was the Roman governor. He was a hard and cruel man and was not concerned with Jewish religious feelings. He normally lived in his palace at Caesarea on the coast, but he came up to Jerusalem to keep order during important festivals such as Passover when the Jews were restless and explosive.

The charge against Jesus would have to be a political one, and strong enough to bring about his death. Pilate had no interest in Jewish religious squabbles. Blasphemy against the Jewish religion or even the Jewish God would not concern him. But a charge that Jesus claimed to be the Messiah or 'King of the Jews' was quite another matter in a land which the Romans controlled. They knew only one king, the Emperor Caesar.

The Jewish leaders accused Jesus of misleading the people and telling them not to pay taxes to the Emperor. They pressed the charge that he claimed to be the Messiah, a king. This was treasonable talk in the ears of the Roman governor. He spoke directly to Jesus: *'Are you the King of the Jews?'* Jesus simply replied: *'So you say'*. He made no claim for himself.

It did not take Pilate long to give his verdict to the assembled priests and their crowd of supporters. *'I find no reason to condemn this man.'* But they insisted all the more that Jesus was stirring up trouble all over the country. *'He began it in Galilee and now he has come here.'*

The very mention of Galilee was enough. It was a notorious trouble spot, but it was not Pilate's business. Galilee was ruled by Herod. By good chance Herod was up in Jerusalem for the Passover Festival. Here, thought Pilate, was a way of getting rid of the whole troublesome business. He would send Jesus to Herod to deal with.

Jesus Is Sent to Herod   Luke 23: 6–12

In all the Gospel stories it is only Luke who tells us that Jesus came before Herod. Herod was very pleased to see Jesus as he had heard a great deal about him. He had been curious to see him for a long time. He was hoping to see Jesus perform a miracle – he seemed to think that he was some kind of clever magician.

Herod asked Jesus many questions, but Jesus stood completely silent. This was the cruel man who had put John the Baptist to death. There was no trusting him. The chief priests and teachers of the Law repeated their accusations. When he could get no reply from Jesus, Herod and his soldiers began to mock him. They put a royal robe on him, to show what they thought of this 'king', and sent him back to Pilate.

Jesus Is Sentenced to Death   Luke 23: 13–25

Jesus came back before Pilate. The governor called together the chief priests, the religious teachers and the people. He said to them: *'You brought this man before me and said that he was corrupting the people. I have examined him here in your presence and I have not found him guilty of any of the crimes you accuse him of. Nor did Herod, for he sent him back to me.'* Pilate was quite clear once again in his judgment. *'This man has done nothing to deserve death. I will have him whipped and let him go.'*

But the crowd would have none of it. *'Kill him!'* they shouted. *'Set Barabbas free for us!'* Barabbas was a criminal who had been put in prison for a riot in the city and for murder. Luke puts little blame on the ruthless and cynical Pilate for what is happening. He puts the responsibility firmly on the Jews. His Gentile readers are to understand that Pilate, the Roman governor, wanted to set Jesus free. Three times he said so.

Pilate appealed to the crowd again, but they were now thoroughly roused against Jesus. *'Crucify him! Crucify him!'* they shouted. Pilate made his final appeal. *'What crime has he committed? I cannot find that he has done anything to deserve death.'* And again he said: *'I will have him whipped and set him free.'*

But the shouting went on, no doubt stirred up by the Jewish religious leaders. The crowd was quite beyond reason now and they called at the top of their voices for Jesus to be crucified. At last they succeeded. Pilate passed sentence of death on Jesus. He set Barabbas free and he handed Jesus over for them to do as they wished. Pilate has been remembered from that day to this for this one thing only. *'Crucified under Pontius Pilate'* is still recited day after day all across the world in the creeds of the Church.

Jesus Is Crucified   Luke 23:26–43

Luke's account of Jesus of Nazareth is by no means a 'success story' in a popular sense. He dwells on Jesus' sufferings and shameful death more than any other part of his life and work. The last hours are filled with mockery and rejection.

Luke tells us that the Roman soldiers led Jesus away to the place of execution. Jesus was probably too weak to carry the heavy cross beam which a victim usually carried on the way to crucifixion. The soldiers were anxious to keep moving. They seized a passer-by named Simon who was a Jewish pilgrim from Cyrene in North Africa attending the Festival in Jerusalem. It is interesting that Luke knows his name and where he came from. Simon was compelled by the soldiers to carry the rough cross bar and follow the condemned man.

A large crowd followed on, eager, as always, to see an execution. Among them were some women who had already begun the death wail. When he heard it, Jesus turned and spoke to them, warning them not to weep for him. Let them weep for themselves and their children. If the Romans do this to one man whom even Pilate declared innocent, what will they do when widespread rebellion blazes out against Rome? Perhaps Luke is thinking here about what did happen to Jerusalem. The day was to come, all too soon, in the year A.D. 70 when there was indeed a rebellion against the Romans. The Romans were quite merciless. They starved the people of Jerusalem into surrender, burnt the Temple to the ground, and destroyed the whole city.

It was the custom to fasten the condemned man to the cross beam and then fix it to the post of wood that stood at the place of execution. The hill where the crosses were set up was well outside the wall of the Holy City. The place itself was called Golgotha (the Aramaic name) or Calvary (the Latin name), meaning 'the Skull', no doubt from its shape.

Two other men were led there to be put to death with Jesus. He was crucified with a criminal on his right and another on his left. Meanwhile the cruelty went on, in the mockery of the crowd, the grim work of the Roman soldiers, the bitter jeers of one of the criminals. Jesus' only words were a cry of prayer to God. *'Father, forgive them. They don't know what they are doing.'* His life showed his trust in God and love for all men. So does his death.

The religious leaders of the Jews were there to see their plans carried out. They jeered at Jesus: *'He saved others; let him save himself if he is God's Messiah!'*

The soldiers divided his clothes among themselves by throwing dice for them. It was their right to take a criminal's last things. They did not know what a Messiah was, but they picked up the mockery of the crowd, noting the words over his head on the cross. *'This is the King of the Jews'*. They called out: *'Save yourself if you are the King of the Jews!'*

One of the criminals hurled insults at Jesus. *'You are the Messiah, are you? Then save yourself and us.'* The other man, however, rebuked him. *'Our sentence is only right, because we are getting what we deserve for what we did; but he has done no wrong.'* The dying man appealed to Jesus: *'Remember me when you come as king!'* Jesus gave an instant reply: *'Today you will be in Paradise with me!'*

The Death of Jesus   Luke 23: 44–49

Jesus was crucified about nine in the morning, the third hour of the Roman day. It was a slow and agonizing death. Luke tells us that at noon the sun stopped shining and darkness covered the whole land for three hours. Perhaps he remembered passages from the Jewish scriptures such as these:

'The day of the Lord is coming . . .
Every star and every constellation will stop shining.
The sun will be dark when it rises, and the moon will give no light.'
(Isaiah 13: 9–10)

'The time is coming when I will make the sun go down at noon and the earth grow dark in daytime.'
(Amos 8:9)

A great deal of ancient literature mentions strange things accompanying the death of famous men.

Luke also mentions that the curtain hanging in the Temple was torn in two. This was the richly coloured linen curtain which screened off the Holy of Holies, the shrine at the very centre of the Temple. The Jews had come to believe that this shrine was in a special sense the house of God. Only the Jewish High Priest was allowed into this room, and only once a year. Luke is using picture language here to say that the life and death of Jesus has given all people everywhere access to God.

Jesus gave a loud cry and called out: *'Father! in your hands I place my spirit!'* The words are an echo from a verse from a Psalm Jesus must have known well:

'I place myself in your care.
You will save me, Lord:
You are a faithful God.'
(Psalm 31:5)

In the Daily Prayer Book for Jews today these words are set down as a goodnight prayer for young children, and also as a confession of trust for the dying.

With these words Jesus died. At this point Luke records a last tribute from the Roman officer in charge of the crucifixion. His words were: *'Certainly he was a good man!'*

The crowd began to drift away. The disciples are not named, but some of Jesus' friends were there, in particular the women from Galilee. They stood at a distance to watch, but there was nothing more to see. Luke mentions the women as a sort of prologue or introduction to what is to follow: the burial of Jesus.

The cross – a challenge to barriers today. Three gigantic crosses set up at Gdansk as a memorial to Poland's workers who died in the clashes with the authorities in 1970.

The Burial of Jesus   Luke 23: 50–56

At the moment of Jesus' death, Luke introduces a man called Joseph from Arimathea, a town in the hill-country of Judaea. He was a wealthy Jew and a member of the Sanhedrin. He was apparently a secret follower of Jesus, and Luke praises him as a good and honourable man. Plainly Joseph had not agreed with the plotting of the other members of the Council. But he was a powerful and determined man. He had the courage to go right into the presence of Pilate to ask for the body of Jesus. He was anxious to give it a decent burial before sunset, the beginning of the Sabbath. Jewish Law was very strict on this point:

> '*A dead body hanging on a post brings God's curse on the land. Bury the body, so that you will not defile the land which the Lord your God is giving you.*'
> (Deuteronomy 21:23)

Joseph took the body down from the cross, wrapped it in a linen sheet and placed it in a tomb cut out of the hillside rock. It was the evening of the day Christians call Good Friday.

The women of Galilee who had been at the cross saw the tomb and how Jesus' body was placed in it. They would know where to come back to. But there was no time before the Sabbath for mourning or for any funeral rites. They went home and prepared spices and perfumes for a later anointing of Jesus' body. Meanwhile the Sabbath was approaching, the day of rest for all Jews.

Christians do not believe that the death of Jesus was the end of the story, and in the next chapter we will explore how they celebrate this belief.

_____TEST YOUR UNDERSTANDING _____

● In our look at 'Christians at Worship' we have already met light as a religious symbol. Draw up two lists, one of the ideas which you associate with light, and the other of the ideas which you associate with darkness.

● What do you think Luke means by saying: 'the sun stopped shining and darkness covered the whole country' when Jesus died?

● How does Luke dramatically put across his belief that the life and death of Jesus has removed the barriers between God and people?

THE CHRISTIAN CALENDAR

□□

5

Holy Days and Holidays

The important events in the life of Jesus are not only written down in the Gospels for us to read. They are also recalled week by week in the services of the Church throughout the world. Each week a particular theme from the life and teaching of Jesus guides the Order of Service – that is, the choice of prayers, hymns, Bible readings and sermon. These themes follow the Calendar of the Christian Year which is kept by all the main branches of the Church.

Our day-to-day pocket diaries and calendars mention Holy days and holidays, such as Christmas and Easter. The Christian Year has many more days to keep – 'red letter days' as they used to be marked in the old calendars. They include not only the main events in the life of Jesus but also important stages in the life of the Church, and the commemoration of famous saints.

The day which marks the beginning of the week for Christians is Sunday. It is a continual reminder of the day on which they believe Jesus rose from the dead and the New Testament calls it 'the Lord's day'. It was the worship day for the believers of the early Church. They met at daybreak for prayer and instruction, the singing of hymns and the breaking of bread.

The full Christian Calendar developed over the six hundred years after the birth of Jesus. Eventually the Calendar took account of Advent, Christmas, Lent, Easter, Ascension Day, Whit Sunday and Trinity Sunday. In addition there were many Saints' Days commemorated by the Church, for example, St Andrew, St Patrick, St George, St David, and the festival of All Saints on November 1, to remember all Christian saints, known or unknown. The Eastern and Western Churches celebrate some of the festivals on different dates, but the main events which they celebrate are the same.

The most important feature of the Christian Year, however, is that all the major events in the life of Jesus are remembered at a particular time of the year so that throughout the course of the year the entire life of Jesus is brought before the worshipper in the prayers, lessons, hymns, sermons and ceremonies of worship. So the 'instruction' of the believer, as the first Christians called it, is always going on.

For all Christians the main festivals are Christmas and Easter. Christmas celebrates the birth of Jesus. Easter commemorates his death and resurrection. Just as their weekly and daily worship gives us insights into what Christians believe to be important, so too do these central festivals of the Christian Year. To find out what these festivals mean to Christians, we shall look at how they are celebrated, and see what stories of Jesus are associated with each of them, and explore the insights into life which Christians claim the festivals offer.

———————————— *Research*————————————

- With the help of calendars and diaries, draw up a Christian Calendar for the current year. List all the festivals and Saints' Days which you have discovered.
- Make use of reference books from the school library to write a short note on each of these special days.

Christmas

Christmas Customs

The Christian Calendar begins at the end of November with the season of Advent. The name Advent literally means 'the coming', and the period of four Sundays leading to Christmas are kept as a time of preparation when Christians think about the meaning of the birth of Jesus. In many homes children learn the Christmas story day by day with the help of an Advent calendar. Each calendar has twenty-four numbered 'windows', one of which is opened each day to reveal a picture, until the whole Christmas story is shown by Christmas Day. Some families burn an Advent candle which has marks down its side to number off the days to Christmas.

Many other customs have grown up about Christmas. The Christmas tree, for example, with its star, tinsel and lights; garlands of holly and ivy and other evergreens; cards to send, presents to wrap up and give and receive; family parties and games and special meals with plum pudding, mince pies and crackers; children hanging up stockings and leaving gifts of food and drink for Santa Claus or Father Christmas.

Christmas customs vary from land to land and from family to family, but some are found all over the world. In churches large and small, in town squares, or even at home, cribs are set up, made of many different materials to

A Christmas tableau at a mission near Johannesburg

picture the Nativity scene. At the centre is the baby Jesus in the manger, watched over by Mary and Joseph. Round about the holy family are the oxen and asses and the shepherds and wise men with their gifts. Angels and the star overhead are symbols to show that God himself was present in the humble inn at Bethlehem. And all round the world the message of Christmas is told and sung at services. There are Bible readings and well-known carols, and members of the congregation light candles to celebrate the birth of Jesus, 'the Light of the world.'

We cannot put an exact date on the first celebration of Christmas by the early Church. Some branches observed it in January, others in the Spring of the year. No one knows the time of year when Jesus was born or even the exact year of his birth. But eventually the Church fixed on the 25th December, perhaps because that was about the time of the winter solstice, the turning-point of the year – 'the birthday of the unconquered sun'. The Roman festival of Saturnalia at that time lasted a week. It was a time of holiday and merrymaking, homes were decorated with evergreens, there were parties and presents and games, and the Christmas tree as we know it dates back to that time. Many of the ancient customs of the pagan festival were adopted by the Christians. As the Christian missionaries spread their message across the world, many other customs and songs have grown up around Christmas.

The early Christians thought it right to associate the birth of Jesus with the turning of the year. The dark winter was behind them, the light of the sun was conquering the darkness of night. Christians thought of Jesus, 'the Light of the world', overcoming all the powers of darkness. The evergreens reminded them of life growing fresh and green in spite of the deadness of winter. Christmas presents recalled the gifts which the wise men brought to the baby Jesus. The Christmas tree was a symbol of the tree of life.

An attractive Christmas symbol which is both ancient and modern is the Christingle, which goes back to Roman times. The Christingle is a decorated orange, a symbol of the world. A candle on the top stands for Jesus, 'the Light of the world'. All over the surface of the orange are small sticks holding fruit and nuts, to represent the fruits of the earth which Christians believe are God's gifts to us. A red ribbon around the orange represents the blood of Jesus. So an old pagan gift of the winter season has become the Christingle, full of Christian meaning.

Carols

The meaning of Christmas is summed up in the Christian word: Incarnation, which literaly means 'in the flesh'.

Some people do not find definitions and religious terms very helpful or meaningful. But from childhood to old age we can remember and understand the stories, songs and customs of Christmas. That is why the best-known T.V. and radio programme in the whole Christian Year is *The Festival of Nine Lessons and Carols* which is usually broadcast from King's College, Cambridge on Christmas Eve. It tells the whole story of Christmas in song and story.

The prayer which opens the programme every year says:

*'Beloved in Christ, be it this Christmastide our care
and delight to prepare ourselves to hear again the
message of the Angels, and in heart and mind to go
even unto Bethlehem, and see this thing which is come
to pass, and the Babe, lying in a manger.'*

Choristers at King's College Chapel, Cambridge

It is the carols which tell the meaning of Christmas best of all:

'Love came down at Christmas,
Love all lovely, Love Divine;
Love was born at Christmas,
Star and angels gave the sign.

Worship we the Godhead,
Love Incarnate, Love Divine;
Worship we our Jesus:
But wherewith for sacred sign?

Love shall be our token,
Love be yours and love be mine,
Love to God and all men,
Love for plea and gift and sign.'

Christina Rossetti

TEST YOUR UNDERSTANDING

- Explain why the Church chose the 25th December as an appropriate date to celebrate the birth of Jesus.
- What is meant by the line in the carol: *'Love shall be our token'*?

Christmas Stories

The Christmas stories of the Gospels are the inspiration for all the beliefs and songs and customs we have been looking at.

Two of the Gospels, Matthew and Luke, tell that Jesus was born in Bethlehem. They open their stories with legendary tales of his birth and infancy. Neither writer is concerned simply with the earthly background of Jesus of Nazareth in ordinary biographical fashion. Certainly Jesus was born and lived and died as a real flesh and blood human being. But these writers' main interest is not in the facts of the birth, life and death, but in their meaning. We can only understand the birth stories of Jesus if we ask the right questions – not: 'What really happened?' but rather: 'What does this mean?' and 'Why did Matthew and Luke want to put it this way?'

Because we are following Luke's Gospel in *Search* we will have to leave behind the wise men, the star and the gifts of gold, myrrh and frankincense, all of which are found only in Matthew's story. If you are able to try some of the suggested Research activities, however, you may come across them then.

Luke's Birth Stories

As we have seen, Luke was a Gentile, not a Jew, and so the stories which he tells about the birth of Jesus are written for Gentiles like himself. The stories also remind us of Luke's interest in the humble, poor, outcast and women, all of whom held an inferior position in Jewish society at that time.

In the first two chapters of Luke's Gospel he sets down a series of poems and religious songs about the birth and infancy of John the Baptist and Jesus set against the historic background of their life and times. These stories remind us of similar Jewish tales in the Old Testament about the birth of Isaac, Samson and especially Samuel, and they probably came to Luke's mind fresh from his knowledge of the sacred scriptures of the Jewish people. The poems and songs have become part of the worship of the Christian Church, known and sung throughout all branches of the Church to this day. You will recognize them as the 'five joyful mysteries of the Rosary' (see page 36). In these opening chapters Luke is not working with a television camera or writing a documentary script. His concern is to tell that this is the work of God from the beginning. The child born at Bethlehem is to be recognized as 'the Son of the Most High God.'

The Dedication of the Gospel   *Luke 1: 1–4*
Luke addresses his Gospel to Theophilus. No one knows who Theophilus was, but he may have been a high-ranking official who was sympathetic to the Christian faith or who had himself become a Christian. It reminds us of the audience for whom Luke was writing.

The Births of John the Baptist and of Jesus Are Announced
Luke presents his stories of the announcement of the births of John the Baptist and of Jesus in almost identical language. In both cases the archangel Gabriel is God's messenger. Zechariah and Elizabeth are mentioned in one story, Joseph and Mary in the other. In both tales the good news is that a son is to be born. It is an early hint of the words which John the Baptist uses at the beginning of his preaching: *'someone is coming who is greater than I am'*.

The Birth of John The Baptist Is Announced   Luke 1: 5–25

Luke opens his story by setting a date on it: it was in the reign of Herod the Great, the ruler appointed by the Romans to be king of Palestine. He goes on to tell of a priestly family, Zechariah and his wife Elizabeth. They were both good and faithful law-abiding Jews. Their one great sorrow was that they had no children. The Jews regarded childlessness as a great evil, probably even a punishment from God.

The priests came up to Jerusalem for a week's service in the Temple, to offer incense at the morning and evening sacrifice at the altar in front of the Holy of Holies while the people waited and prayed outside. There were so many priests that they were chosen by lot for this sacred task, and each one had one chance only to make the incense offering. Some of them were never chosen at all, so this must have been the greatest moment in Zechariah's life.

At the sight of the archangel Gabriel, Zechariah was alarmed and afraid. Gabriel's message is full of joy: *'your wife Elizabeth will bear a son. You are to name him John'*. The name means 'God has been gracious'. The child is to be a great man in the story of God's people, the Jews. He is to be strong and mighty like the prophet Elijah who Jews believe did not die but was carried off to heaven in a fiery chariot. This is Luke's reminder to his readers that according to Jewish tradition Elijah is to come again to prepare the way for the Messiah.

As a sign and a punishment for his lack of faith, Gabriel tells the doubting Zechariah that he will be struck dumb until the day that the promise comes true. And so, of course, it comes to pass.

The Birth of Jesus Is Announced   Luke 1: 26–38

In close parallel comes the story of the announcement of the forthcoming birth of Jesus. There is constant repetition in both stories of the sense of joy. This time God sends his angel Gabriel to a town in Galilee named Nazareth. Again Luke mentions both adults: Joseph and Mary. He reminds us that Joseph was a descendant of King David. The angel appears to the woman this time, to Mary who is a girl promised in marriage to Joseph. He tells her that she will give birth to a son who is to be named Jesus. The name means 'God is salvation'. It is the Greek form of the Hebrew name Joshua. He will be a true descendant of David and inherit his royal throne and kingdom. This expresses the longings and prayers of many generations of Jews. The child to be born will be the Son of God. This, as we have seen, is a theme which Luke pursues all through his Gospel. At this point there is a direct mention of the Virgin Birth. Mary says: *'I am a virgin. How can this be?'* The angel's reply is that it will all come about through the Holy Spirit of God – another theme of particular interest to Luke. Mary bows humbly at the news: *'I am the Lord's servant, may it happen to me as you have said'*.

Mary Visits Elizabeth   Luke 1: 39–56

Mary went to visit Elizabeth. The importance of this short passage lies in Elizabeth's words: *'You are the most blessed of all women, and blessed is the child you will bear'*. Even the unborn child stirring in Elizabeth's womb acknowledges the importance of Mary and her son-to-be. Already Luke calls Jesus 'my Lord'.

We come to 'Mary's Song of Praise' which has become famous in Church tradition as the Magnificat, or 'Hymn of Mary'. The song is a close parallel of the song of Hannah at the birth of Samuel in the Old Testament, and was no doubt suggested to Luke by that passage. (See 1 Samuel 2: 1–10)

The Magnificat has been used in the worship of the Church for many centuries, and has often been set to beautiful music. For all that, it is no lullaby. It is one of the most revolutionary songs the world has ever known.

> 'He has stretched out his mighty arm
> and scattered the proud with all their plans.
> He has brought down mighty kings
> from their thrones,
> and lifted up the lowly.
> He has filled the hungry with good things,
> and sent the rich away with empty hands.'

In this song Luke strikes the note of deep sympathy with the humble and poor which, as we have seen, is a major theme of his Gospel.

The Birth of John the Baptist   Luke 1: 57–66

Once again there is the note of joy when Elizabeth gives birth to her son. It is now that the name John is given, and Zechariah's power of speech comes back to him. The theme of the passage is of wonder and fear at the work of God. *'What is this child going to be?'*

Zechariah's Prophecy   Luke 1: 67–80

There follows another of Luke's songs which is usually known as 'The Song of Zechariah' or the Benedictus. It is full of memories of Old Testament hopes and promises of a deliverer who will set God's people free. He is to be a descendant of the great King David and will *'rescue us from our enemies.'*

It is a very Jewish song, and does not at all closely fit the life of Jesus, still less his sufferings and death. Nor does it take account of Luke's interest in the wider Gentile world. The early church had eventually to think out the fact that Jesus did not fulfil the narrow hopes of a political Messiah. To this day, however, this song is used in the traditional worship of the Church.

The song concludes by coming back to John. He grew up and lived in the wilderness. It was the traditional background for a prophet.

The Birth of Jesus   Luke 2: 1–20

Now that Luke has set the scene with his poems and songs about the birth of John, he turns to the story of the birth of Jesus. In spite of the fact that he mentions Caesar Augustus in the opening sentence, we must always keep in mind that most of the material in the opening chapters of Luke's Gospel belongs not to the world of history and geography, but to the world of symbolism and meaning. There is no evidence outside the Bible for a census which took place in the whole Roman Empire, but a local census was not uncommon. In any case, Luke wants to set the humble birth of Jesus against the background of the great and mighty Empire. His Gospel, as we have seen, was written for Gentiles, citizens of that Roman world.

Joseph is mentioned again as a descendant of the royal house of David, and Mary is promised in marriage to him. They travel from the town of Nazareth in

Galilee to Bethlehem, which was a few miles from Jerusalem in Judaea. The significance of Bethlehem is that it was the birth place of David. The inn was crowded, so the part of the building usually used for the animals at night had to make do for these humble visitors. Mary wrapped her first-born son in swaddling-clothes and laid him in the straw-filled manger, the animals' feeding trough. So Luke shows us the humble beginning of his Jesus' story.

The theme is further stressed in Luke's tale of the visitors to the manger, the shepherds, lowliest of men. According to Luke's legend they were in the fields by night looking after their flocks when an angel of the Lord appeared to them. The good news is of a saviour born in David's town. He is the long-promised Messiah. The proof will be, so they are told, that they will find a baby wrapped in bits of cloth, lying in a manger.

The rejoicing at the birth is emphasised by a great choir of angels singing praises to God. The song of the angels is yet another hymn of the Christian Church which has been repeated all down the ages. The shepherds hurry to Bethlehem and find Mary and Joseph, and see the baby lying in the manger. They tell their story of the angels and then go back to their work, singing praises to God.

This chapter is the basis of many Christmas cards and poems and famous works of art. Good news, joy, peace on earth are key-words of the whole passage.

Two 'charity' Christmas cards which reflect Luke's story and its contemporary relevance.

Jesus Is Presented in the Temple   Luke 2: 21–40

According to Jewish custom, the child Jesus was circumcised on the eighth day after birth and was given the name Jesus. Luke now turns to Jerusalem, the ancient capital of the Jews, the city where David had once reigned. The Law of Moses stated God's command: *'Dedicate all the first-born males to me.'* So Joseph and Mary took the child to Jerusalem where the Temple was the centre of worship. Their offering for the purification of the mother was two young pigeons, according to the tradition of the Law for poor people.

70

It is at this point that Luke introduces his legend of Simeon and Anna to draw attention to the importance of this Jewish child. Simeon is a symbolic figure of the finest Jewish tradition, a 'good devout man' who was waiting and praying for the coming of God's promised Messiah. The whole story implies that God is at work. It is God who preserves Simeon in old age and guides him into the Temple on this special day when the parents bring the child Jesus. So Simeon, led by the Spirit of God, takes the child in his hands and gives thanks.

The 'Song of Simeon' as it is sometimes called, or Nunc Dimittis in its Latin title, is a regular part of worship in all the main branches of the Church.

Simeon's words to Mary speak not of a triumphant, kingly Messiah, but of one who will mysteriously bring about destruction and sorrow as well as salvation. The poem reminds us strongly of the words of one of the great Jewish prophets:

'The glory of the Lord will be revealed,
and all mankind will see it.
The Lord himself has promised this.'
(Isaiah 40:5)

'I, the Lord, have called you and given you power
to see that justice is done on earth.
through you I will make a covenant with all peoples;
through you I will bring light to the nations.'
(Isaiah 42:6)

The other person in Luke's story at this point is Anna, 'a very old prophetess'. She is the female counterpart of Simeon, a faithful worshipper in the Temple. Anna, too, gives thanks to God for the child.

Luke ends his birth stories by saying that Joseph and Mary go back to Nazareth.

The Boy Jesus in the Temple   *Luke 2: 41–52*
This is the only story in all the gospels about the boyhood of Jesus, and it is told as a story full of meaning. Luke says that the parents of Jesus went to Jerusalem every year for the Passover Festival, the chief event of the Jewish calendar. It was the busiest time of the year in the Holy City and every corner was crowded with pilgrims. The point of the story is that Jesus at the age of twelve became 'a son of the Law' as every Jewish boy still does about that age. At the bar-mitzvah ceremony, as it is called, he becomes an adult in Jewish eyes, taking on himself the religious duties and responsibilities of manhood and personal obedience to the Law.

The main point of Luke's tale, however, lies in what follows. When his parents turned homewards after the week-long festival, Jesus stayed in Jerusalem. Eventually Joseph and Mary search anxiously for him, first among their relatives and friends on the crowded highway, then back to the busy city. They find him in the Temple, sitting with the Jewish teachers, *'listening to them and asking questions.'* When his worried mother spoke to him, Jesus replied: *'Didn't you know that I had to be in my Father's house?'* This is the climax of Luke's story. He is once again reminding his readers that here we have no ordinary Jewish boy, but one who is Son of God in a special sense. At the moment which marks the beginning of his manhood, Jesus is aware of God as his Father. It is, as we have seen, something which runs all through Luke's Gospel.

Luke brings all his birth and infancy stories to an end by saying that Jesus returned to Nazareth with Joseph and Mary and grew in body and in wisdom and in favour with God and man. This peaceful summary is a contrast to the tale of controversy and suffering which is to follow throughout Jesus' later life.

TEST YOUR UNDERSTANDING

- In what ways is the story of the announcement of the birth of Jesus similar to the story of the announcement of the birth of John the Baptist? Why does Luke present these as parallel stories?
- Copy down the words from the story of Mary's visit to Elizabeth which help to explain the importance given to Mary in the Orthodox and Roman Catholic Churches.
- State in your own words how God is pictured in the *Magnificat*.
- Copy out Luke 1: 75 in your own words. To what extent do you think that this is a good summary of true religion?
- How does Luke show that God was present at the birth of Jesus?
- How does Luke's story of the birth of Jesus reflect his concern for the poor and humble?
- Which verse in the *Nunc Dimittis* reflects Luke's belief that Jesus is both Jewish Messiah and 'Saviour of all mankind'?
- Why does Luke include the story of Jesus' *bar-mitzvah* ceremony?

_____ *Research* _____

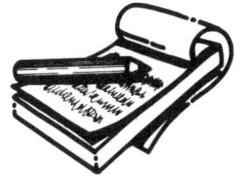

- Collect as many Christmas cards as possible and group them as follows:
  1. those which reflect Luke's story;
  2. those which reflect Matthew's story, which can be found in Matthew 2: 1–12;
  3. those which combine elements of both stories;
  4. others.
- List any ways in which the cards in groups 1 and 2 change the original stories. Do any of these changes reflect twentieth-century concerns or interests?
- Do you consider the popular version of the Christmas story as shown in group 3 to be more helpful or more misleading than the original separate stories? Explain your answer.
- Study the cards in group 4. State any motifs (candles, bells, robins, etc.) which occur again and again, and try to explain the reasons for this. What percentage of the cards in this group do you consider to be completely irrelevant to the message of Christmas?
- Identify and describe the card from any of the groups which you consider best communicates the Christmas message for twentieth-century people.
  or
  Design your own Christmas card to communicate the Christmas message to the twentieth century.

Christmas Today

CHRISTMAS FAST

A fast at Christmas to benefit the starving of the Third World was launched in Edinburgh yesterday. Participants in "Fast Aid" are asked to fast on one of the twelve days of Christmas and give the money saved to the hungry.

The Glasgow Herald 8/11/86

Bethlehem

Pilgrims sang "Silent Night" in the Church of the Nativity as hundreds of visitors, guarded by Israeli troops gathered for Christmas festivities at the traditional birthplace of Jesus.

The Glasgow Herald 24/12/86

SERVE THOSE WHO STAND IN NEED OF FRIENDSHIP

A message from the Moderator of the General Assembly of the Church of Scotland.

There are many ways in which darkness plays a great part in the Christmas story. We love to hold candlelit services in church where the true effect is felt only when the electric lights are shut off. Our decorated trees look so much better in the dark when the coloured lights are seen to full effect. Christmas is a festival of light. It comes at the darkest time of the year and I believe there is a message in that – a message of hope, that in spite of the darkness which exists in the lives of so many of our fellow citizens there is in God's plan a way of light as opposed to a way of darkness for the world.

Look at the world today – Aids, drugs and alcohol abuse, political corruption, the breakdown of family life, child abuse. This is the darkness of the world. The message at Christmas is that there is an alternative to all of these. They are not inevitable. None of them is sent by God. They are a consequence of man's disobedience to God's will but they are not divine punishment.

As against this darkness we look to the gospels and the light that came into the world and continues to shine on all mankind. Today, as at the first Christmas, people are looking for a liberator. It is a great time for us all. Even the exchange of Christmas cards indicates a remembrance of each other. It draws people together and families are reunited.

In the midst of the goodwill and generosity of spirit engendered by Christmas we should pause and think of the large numbers of people for whom the prospects of Christmas and the months ahead seem very dark and bleak.

If we are to celebrate this season of Christ in a Christian fashion it is not enough just to recognise the call to worship. We are simultaneously called to the service of our fellow men. We should go out of our way to be of service to people perhaps of a race, class, or religion other than our own, who stand in need of ordinary human friendship. There are more of them on our doorsteps than most of us realise. If we can find room and time for God and for them in this time, we shall have come closer to celebrating Christmas in spirit and in truth.

The Glasgow Herald 24/12/86

TEST YOUR UNDERSTANDING

- How do the two short reports illustrate the 'call of worship' and the 'call to the service of our fellow men'?
- What evidence does the Moderator give of 'the darkness of the world'?
- According to the Moderator, what is the message of Christmas?
- How should Christians celebrate Christmas?

Easter

Easter Customs

The Date
The Calendar of the Christian Year begins with Advent and leads to Chri:tmas. But the oldest and most important festival of the Christian Year is Easter, which commemorates the resurrection of Jesus. The date of Easter is not fixed, like other important days in the Christian Year. It depends on the time of the full moon in the Spring of the year, and may fall on any date from 22nd March to 25th April.

Lent
The solemn nature of the Easter season is marked by forty weekdays and six Sundays of preparation, known as Lent. Lent is a very old name for the lengthening days of spring and it runs from Ash Wednesday to the Saturday before Easter day. The last seven days of Lent are known as Holy Week.

During Lent Christians recall the forty days Jesus spent fasting in the wilderness before he began his life's work. It has always been observed in the Church as a time of preparation and fasting and prayer. In the early centuries of the Church the fast of Lent was very strictly kept, with no meat or fish and only one meal a day. Nowadays many Christians give up luxuries and spend time in prayer and seriously consider how to live a more charitable and self-sacrificing life. In some churches purple cloth or even sackcloth is used to stress the solemn and important nature of Lent.

Shrove Tuesday
The day before the season of Lent begins is known as Shrove Tuesday or Pancake Tuesday. People used to go to church before Lent to make confession of their sins and be 'shriven', that is, receive forgiveness. The name 'Shrove' comes from that ancient act of confession and forgiveness.

The other title for the day, Pancake Tuesday, arose because everyone had to use up their rich food before the days of fasting began. Making pancakes was a good way of using up eggs and butter and other fats. It was also a last burst of merrymaking before the solemn days of Lent. Some towns still observe a race on Pancake Tuesday, with housewives and girls tossing their homemade pancakes as they run. In France there is a famous carnival called Mardi Gras – which means 'Fat Tuesday' – and the carnival custom has spread to many other lands.

Ash Wednesday
Lent begins on Ash Wednesday. The ash, which is an age-old sign of mourning, comes from burning the palm crosses which were blessed on the previous year's Palm Sunday. The priest sprinkles the ashes with holy water and makes a mark on the worshipper's head.

A prayer for Ash Wednesday is:

'Lord, protect us in our struggle against evil.
As we begin the discipline of Lent,
make this day holy by our self-denial.'

the coracle

THE NEWSPAPER OF THE IONA COMMUNITY

No. 10   **FEBRUARY-MARCH 1983**   15p

A Fast For Freedom

LENT — what do you do with it? Traditional ways of observing this penitential season — giving things up, fasting — are not always satisfactory. According to Isaiah, the fast the Lord wants is "to let the oppressed go free, to break every yoke, to share your bread with the hungry, and bring the homeless poor into your house." Below are 40 suggestions — one for each day of Lent (which begins on Ash Wednesday, 16th February). Pin this Coracle front page up on your wall and try the ideas. After this Lent, your life may never be the same . . .

1 Fast for 12 hours for Ash Wednesday. Meditate: Amos 5 v21-24.

2 Wear a peace badge *from now on.*

3 Go and see the film "Gandhi" — then spin for 20 hours.

4 Bake a cake and take it to someone you have disagreed with.

5 Prayer meditation on the Sermon on the Mount.

6 Write a letter to Mrs Thatcher, Michael Heseltine; kiss a policeman/woman.

7 Design and make a banner.

8 Send a photo of your family to a church or peace group in the Soviet Union.

9 Invite friends to a rich/poor meal.

10 Buy a new book on disarmament or development *and read it.*

11 Arrange the showing of a video, film or slide-tape, on peace and development issues.

12 Hold a silent vigil somewhere appropriate. Meditate: Psalm 139.

13 Go into a shop and explain why you are *not* buying Nestle's or Outspan.

14 Write a letter to your MP, or arrange to see him/her.

15 Invite the next-door neighbour in and talk about disarmament.

16 Pay your CND/Parents for Survival subscription, or subscribe to Sojourners or Peace News.

17 Sing for peace — either in your local church or in the street.

18 Visit a peace camp, or send something they need, or write.

19 Join a peace blockade, or pray for those who are blockading. Meditation: Luke 6 v47-49.

20 Walk to work — within reason. Read about Martin Luther King's bus boycott.

21 Display a peace, development poster in your window.

22 Fast for a day and give the food money to Christian Aid. Invite others to join in with poems, etc. Meditate: Matthew 6 v16-18.

23 Smile before breakfast . . . smile again after breakfast!

24 Start training for marathon.

25 Run a bookstall at your local church, market, place of work.

26 Study one of the Churches Council's "Choose Life" topics. Meditate: Leviticus 25 and 26. Jubilee.

27 Sell some bags of Campaign Coffee or WDM tea.

28 Write to local newspapers on a current development, disarmament topic.

29 Send an application for the Non-Violence or the Development Week on Iona.

30 Invite overseas friends to an international pot-luck meal.

31 Check up on your recycling, and take jumble to the nearest jumble sale.

32 Collect signatures for a peace petition.

33 Study and pray about the Iona Peace Conference's worship for the Good Friday service at the Ministry of Defence.

34 Send a donation to Centrepeace, or visit your local Third World shop, and support it.

35 Write to a church group or peace group in the USA.

36 Play a poverty game with the children.

37 Write to a Bishop of the Church of England Synod about "The Church and the Bomb".

38 Paint your Easter eggs with peace signs and give them away.

39 Find your nearest bunker or missile base and leaflet outside it about civil defence.

40 Hold a Palm Sunday service of commitment to the way of peace. Meditate: Luke 4 v18-19.

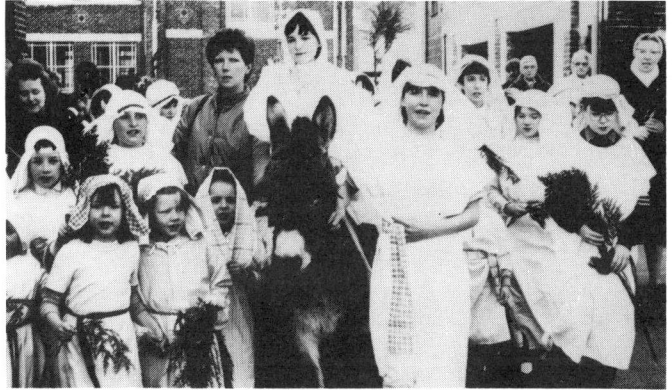

A donkey leads the way in a children's procession for Palm Sunday

Palm Sunday

The Sunday before Easter is Palm Sunday, which marks the beginning of Holy Week, the time when Christians especially remember the suffering and death of Jesus. Many churches are decorated with palm branches, willows and other green leaves and the whole congregation carries branches and joins in a procession to represent Jesus' triumphal entry into Jerusalem. The worshippers also bring small crosses of dried palm leaves to be blessed by the priest. A familiar hymn in all branches of the Church on this Sunday is:

'All glory, laud and honour
To thee, Redeemer King,
To whom the lips of children
Made sweet hosannas ring!'

In many churches services are held every day during Holy Week. Nowadays Christians from different traditions often unite in worship at this time.

Maundy Thursday

Thursday of Holy Week is known as Maundy Thursday. The name 'Maundy' comes from the Latin *mandatum,* meaning 'command', and is a reminder of Jesus' words to his disciples at the Last Supper: *'Now I give you a new com-mandment: love one another. As I have loved you, so you must love one another'.*

In St Peter's Cathedral in Rome every Maundy Thursday, the Pope washes the feet of twelve people while great crowds gather to watch. This ritual, which is repeated in many local Roman Catholic churches, is an acting out of the story John's Gospel tells, that Jesus washed his disciples' feet before they all joined together in the Last Supper:

'He rose from the table, took off his outer garment, and tied a towel round his waist. Then he poured some water into a basin and began to wash his disciples' feet and dry them with the towel round his waist.' (John 13: 4 - 5).

The service is an object-lesson in humility and self-giving, a reminder that Jesus said: *'I have set an example for you, so that you will do just what I have done for you.'* Church services on the Thursday evening of Holy Week also remind Christians of the Last Supper and the events which followed it when Jesus was arrested in the Garden of Gethsemane.

Good Friday

On Good Friday many churches have a continual three-hour service from noon to three o'clock to commemorate the hours Jesus hung on the cross. As well as hymns and prayers, there are usually short sermons on the seven sayings of Jesus from the cross. In Roman Catholic churches there is the ritual of 'venerating the cross', in which the priests and people kneel in silence and bow before the cross or kiss it, in memory of the death of Jesus. A very old Good Friday custom which is widely observed is the eating of spicy hot cross buns.

Easter Day

At midnight on the Saturday of Holy Week the long theme of preparation in Lent comes to an end, and Easter begins. Easter morning is a time of great joy, the climax to weeks of meditation and prayer and self-denial. Worshippers often wear new clothes to celebrate the day and they adorn the church with bright Spring flowers in white and yellow and gold. Many of the Easter hymns are the oldest songs of praise of the Church and they are full of joy and thanksgiving.

One of the oldest traditions of Easter Day is the giving of Easter eggs. The children's game of rolling eggs down a hill is supposed to be in remembrance of the rolling away of the big stone from the tomb where the body of Jesus lay.

In Roman Catholic churches during the Easter Vigil a huge candle, known as the Paschal candle, is lit and carried through the darkened church and worshippers light their own candles from it until pew upon pew is bright with flickering light. Their song is:

'Christ our light.
Thanks be to God!'

A message for Easter and for the world is behind the egg

The Reformed Churches have their own varied ways of keeping Easter. One of the commonest customs is to hold an open-air service at dawn, often on a hill-top, followed by an Easter breakfast which everyone shares. Almost all churches have a service of Holy Communion on Easter morning.

The most exciting Easter celebration of all, and probably the oldest, is in the Orthodox Church. It is 'The Feast of Feasts'. Here is how the celebrations are described by a member of the Orthodox community:

'On the afternoon of Good Friday, a slow procession makes its way from the altar to the centre of the church. The priest or bishop solemnly carries a cloth on which is painted or embroidered an icon of the dead Christ. He lowers it on to a stand in the middle of the building. As at an ordinary funeral, people stand with lighted candles. They bow before the icon and they kiss it.

Later the icon is taken in procession round the outside of the church, with the worshippers following as mourners, while the bells are tolled. The cloth is brought back to the centre of the church to mark the burial itself.

But the burial is not the end of the story. Already at this service (late Friday evening or early Saturday morning) some of the readings and chants hint at the resurrection to come. These hints grow more insistent at the Eucharist on Saturday morning. Up until now the clergy have been wearing solemn, black vestments. Just before the Gospel reading these are suddenly exchanged for festive white ones. And the Gospel itself speaks already of the women at the tomb of Christ who find it empty, and their Saviour risen.

At midnight, in the first moments of Easter Day, this story is taken up again. Just as the women came to the tomb, so clergy and people come in procession to the church. They circle the building and pause before the main doors of the building, which are closed.

The mystery of Christ's tomb is about to be revealed. But for the moment the closed doors represent the great stone which the women at the tomb expected to bar their entrance.

Inside the church the icon of the buried Christ has already been removed to the altar.

Outside, with candles flickering in the cool night air, the people wait for the minister to give the blessing. And then they hear, three times repeated, the triumphant announcement of Christ's victory over death: "Christ is risen from the dead: By death he has trampled down death: And to those who are in the grave he has given life."

The people repeat the chant. Bells are pealed. In some countries sirens join in, guns are fired and fireworks are exploded.

The doors swing open. The procession sweeps in. It is a moment of enormous joy. And the source of that joy is indicated over and over again. Throughout the next part of the service, and throughout the Easter season, Orthodox Christians greet each other cheerfully with the words: "Christ is risen!", and with the answer to this greeting: "Risen indeed"!'

TEST YOUR UNDERSTANDING

- Explain why the day before Lent is called:
  a. Shrove Tuesday
  b. Pancake Tuesday
- Describe the custom associated with Ash Wednesday, and explain its meaning.
- Rewrite the Ash Wednesday prayer in your own words.
- Describe how Christians celebrate the beginning of Holy Week.
- Describe the ritual performed during Holy Week which reminds Christians of Jesus' command to *'love one another'*.
- Describe briefly how Orthodox, Roman Catholic and Reformed Churches celebrate Easter. In your answers concentrate on the meaning and symbolism of the celebrations.

Easter Stories

The Resurrection   *Luke 24: 1–12*

The previous chapter ended with the story of Jesus' death and burial. It is now the day we know as Sunday, the first day of the Jewish week. The sacred Sabbath was over, when no good Jew was to work or travel. Very early in the morning, as soon as it was light to see, the women followers of Jesus were free to go to the tomb. They took with them the spices they had prepared for the last funeral rites, the anointing of the dead body.

A large stone had been rolled over the entrance of the tomb to seal it off. The women, surprised to see that the stone was rolled aside, went into the tomb. But it was empty; they did not find the body of Jesus.

They stood there, puzzled about all this. Had the body been stolen, or what had happened? Suddenly two men in shining clothes stood by them. We are reminded here of the angels which appear in Luke's story of the birth of Jesus.

The empty cross – symbol of the resurrection

Luke wishes to stress in a dramatic manner the presence and activity of God in the events surrounding both the birth and death of Jesus. Just as the angels' message in Luke's birth is of Good News, so too is the message here. *'Why are you looking among the dead for one who is alive? He is not here; he has been raised.'* It was to remind them of Jesus' own teaching, which they had probably forgotten: *'The Son of Man must be handed over to sinful men, be crucified, and three days later rise to life.'*

The women turned away from the empty tomb and came back to Jerusalem to tell the disciples and Jesus' other followers all that they had seen.

But the disciples found their story incredible. Jesus was dead, and that was that. Peter, however, went to see for himself. He ran to the tomb, bent down, and went inside. He saw the linen clothes which had wrapped the body of Jesus, but nothing else. No body, dead or alive. Slowly Peter made his way back to Jerusalem, amazed, and not understanding what had happened.

The Walk to Emmaus   Luke 24: 13 - 35

This long, detailed resurrection story is found only in Luke's Gospel. That same first day of the week, two of Jesus' followers – perhaps man and wife – were on the road to a village named Emmaus, about seven miles from Jerusalem. They were discussing all that had happened, and arguing about it. As they talked, Jesus joined them and went with them, but they did not recognize him. He asked them: *'What are you talking about as you walk along?'*

One of them, whose name was Cleopas, asked the stranger if he had not heard about what had happened in Jerusalem during the last few days. Then they told him about Jesus and his crucifixion.

When he had finished, Jesus asked them: *'Was it not necessary for the Messiah to suffer?'* Their unspoken answer would certainly have been: 'Impossible!' The Messiah was always portrayed as a royal, victorious leader. Jesus had a different way of thinking about himself and his destiny.

The travellers came to the village to which they were going and begged Jesus to stay with them. As they sat at their evening meal, Jesus became the host, not the guest. He took the bread and said the blessing, then he broke the bread and gave it to them. In that familiar act their eyes were opened and they recognized him, and

Giving hands and receiving hands

at that moment he disappeared from their sight. They got up at once and went back to Jerusalem to tell the eleven disciples and the others what had happened on the road and how they had recognized Jesus when he broke the bread.

Luke's story of the walk to Emmaus is full of meaning. Once again the reader is reminded that Jesus was not the Messiah of popular hopes, but one whose vocation was to suffer and die. They have to read and understand the Jewish Scriptures in a new way to see how they were fulfilled in Jesus.

For Luke, Jesus is no longer limited to time and place – he can come and go at will. Luke now names him 'the Lord' which was, and is, the title the risen Jesus has always held among Christians. Most important of all, it is in the breaking of bread that the believer is to recognize his Lord. It early became, and remained, the central and most sacred act of the Christian Church: *'the bread we break: when we eat it we are sharing in the body of Christ'*. (I Corinthians 10: 16)

Jesus Appears to His Disciples   Luke 24: 36 - 49

As the two were telling their story to the others in Jerusalem, the Lord himself suddenly stood among them. He gave his greeting: *'Peace be with you'*. They were terrified, thinking it was a ghost. But Jesus said: *'Why are you alarmed? Look at my hands and feet and see that it is really me. Feel me, and you will know, for a ghost does not have flesh and bones, as you see I have!'*

They were all so full of joy and wonder that they still could not believe. So Jesus asked them for something to eat. They gave him a piece of fish which he took and ate. It is hard to understand Luke's meaning here. At one moment he pictures Jesus coming through closed doors and appearing and disappearing like a ghost. At the next he stresses that it is a flesh and blood Jesus who is present and to emphasize it he pictures him eating a piece of fish. It is as if Luke wants to make it clear that the resurrection is beyond human understanding.

Once again their Lord speaks of the meaning of the Scriptures as if this is by far the most essential matter they must grasp. He tells them they are witnesses of these things that have happened. They have a mission to tell all nations. Meanwhile, they are to wait in Jerusalem until God acts again, sending his power on them.

Jesus Is Taken up to Heaven   Luke 24: 50 - 53

The Gospel of Luke ends with the moment when Jesus leads his friends out of the city on the familiar road to Bethany, on the Mount of Olives. There he lifted his hands and blessed them, and departed from them. His followers went back to Jerusalem filled with joy and spent all their time in the Temple, giving thanks to God. Luke's Gospel begins and ends in the Temple.

_____ **TEST YOUR UNDERSTANDING** _____

- How does Luke make clear that God was really present during the women's visit to the tomb?
- Why do you think the early Christians would read the story of the walk to Emmaus when they celebrated the Eucharist or Holy Communion?
- Which emotions and feelings does Luke stress most in his last two resurrection stories? How are these emotions and feelings recalled in the words and actions of Christians at Easter services today?

Easter Today

Pope's message decries terrorism

Pope John Paul, delivering his Easter message to more than two hundred and fifty thousand people in St. Peter's Square, today decried terrorism, guerrilla warfare and human rights violations. Security appeared tight as the Pope held Mass on the Roman Catholic Church's feast day to mark Christ's resurrection from the dead. In his traditional "Urbi et Orbi" (to the city and the world) message after the Mass, the Pontiff referred to continued conflicts in the world.

"Man resigns himself to death when he aspires to the things of the Earth," the Pope said in a vibrant voice in the message televised live to many parts of the world.

"Yes. Man unfortunately resigns himself to death and not only accepts it but also inflicts it. Men continuously inflict death upon others, people who are often unknown, innocent people, people not yet born," he said.

The Pope, who wore white and gold vestments, said: "Man not only resigns himself to death but he has often made death the method of his existence on earth."

The Pontiff said God called on man to oppose death "in the regions bloodied by guerrilla warfare and conflicts, where there arise temptations to use terrorism and reprisals, in the nations where the dignity of the person, his rights and his freedoms are trampled upon."

The Pope asked whether modern man was ready to share "God's great uprising against death" symbolised by Christ's resurrection after his crucifixion. Man was "faced with a challenge, one more pressing and demanding than all others: the great challenge of peace."

He mentioned his invitation to world religious leaders to pray for peace this year at the Italian town of Assisi, saying it would be an opportunity to confirm the victory of life.

The Glasgow Herald 3/3/86

RUNCIE POINTS TO LESSON IN RAPE CASE

The Archbishop of Canterbury, Dr Robert Runcie yesterday condemned violence against women and children but said Christians must forgive their enemies.

He urged everyone to follow the "impressive example" of a congregation at Ealing, West London, where a vicar and another man were badly beaten and a woman raped during an incident at the vicarage. "We are to love and forgive our enemies and pray for our persecutors – however trying that may be," Dr Runcie said in his Easter Day sermon at Canterbury Cathedral.

"We've seen a fine and impressive example of this quiet Easter faith shining through personal tragedy in a Christian congregation in Ealing.

"Such heroic healing power could hardly fail to move the most determined cynic.

Dr Runcie warned: "We are confronted, at home and abroad, by the dark demonic dimensions of human nature, which can cause the most resilient spirit to quake and shiver.

Christians must be the sworn foes of vicious assault, callous cruelty, persecution, poverty and powerlessness, he said.

"As we watch or read the news we are constantly sickened by sights and first-hand accounts of violence against women and children, against whole groups of people who are labelled and despised."

Violent acts or words would not solve the problems, Dr Runcie said. "The sickness is in the hearts and minds of men and women."

The Archbishop said Christians must care about freedom and justice, but his main message was one of forgiveness.

"Easter is the Good Shepherd coming back to seek and save what is lost." It was about "being found, healed, restored, forgiven."

The Glasgow Herald 31/3/86

TEST YOUR UNDERSTANDING

- Pope John Paul states 'Man . . . has often made death the method of his existence on earth.'
  What evidence does he give to support this statement?
- What does the Pope mean by 'God's great uprising against death'?
- How does he suggest people should share in this 'uprising'?
- The Archbishop of Canterbury refers to 'the dark demonic dimensions of human nature'
  What examples does he give of this?
- What teaching of Jesus does he quote in his Easter message?
  What example does he give of this being put into practice?
- Explain in your own words what, according to the Archbishop, Easter is about.

PERSONAL MILESTONES

6

Just as there are red letter days celebrating the key events in the life of Jesus and of the Church, so there are special days on which the key events in the lives of individuals are remembered and celebrated. These key events are: joining the Christian Church; marriage; death. Each of them is an important personal milestone in the lives of Christians in all three main branches of the Church. The ceremonies and in particular the promises associated with these events tell us more about the Christian answers to our four questions:

Where do we come from:
What are we?
Where are we going?
How do we get there?

Joining the Christian Church

There are three rituals or special ceremonies associated with membership of the Church. These ceremonies are: baptism, confirmation, and first communion. They are found in all three branches of the Church: Orthodox, Roman Catholic, Reformed. Orthodox and Roman Catholic Christians believe that these rituals are sacraments. The Church of Scotland, in common with many of the other Reformed Churches, also regards baptism and communion as sacraments, but not confirmation. As you study this chapter, note the similarities and differences within the three traditions of the Church.

The Orthodox Church

The 'initiation rites' of the Orthodox Church have changed little in a thousand years and more. They go back to a time when people joined the Church as adults

'We heard you had a new way of doing things!'

rather than children, as the words of the ceremonies show. Today the words are spoken on behalf of children by a sponsor or godparent.

As Christianity spread in the early days it became the main religion in many countries. Christian parents naturally wished to bring their children up within the Church. But only in the Orthodox tradition were the three parts of the initiation ceremonies kept together. In the other traditions, although children were baptized as infants, confirmation and first communion took place at later stages.

Baptism

The rituals surrounding the initiation ceremonies in the Orthodox Church are rich in meaning. The priest begins with prayers in which he asks that the child may come to know God and his commandments and in which he orders Satan to come out of the child. The infant's clothes are then taken off as a sign that he is putting away his old self. The priest then turns the child to face the West, from where darkness comes, according to Orthodox belief. The child is asked if he has given up Satan. The sponsor replies on his behalf.

The priest then turns the child to the East, which is the source of light, and the child is asked to confess his belief in Christ. Again the sponsor speaks for him. The priest then recites the Nicene Creed. He puts on special white vestments and lights tapers as a sign of the child 'seeing the light' about Jesus.

Water and oil are then blessed by the priest and he anoints the child with 'the oil of gladness'. Again the priest faces the East and lowers the child under the water three times, while he recites the following words:

> 'The servant of God (giving the child his name) is baptized in the name of the Father, Amen. And of the Son, Amen. And of the Holy Spirit, AMEN.'

An Eastern Orthodox baptism in Crete

Dipping under the water is a sign of the child being 'buried with Christ'. Being lifted out of the water is a sign of his 'rising with Christ'.

As the child is being dried, Psalm 32 is sung, beginning with the words: *'Happy are those whose sins are forgiven, whose wrongs are pardoned'*.

The priest then dresses the child in a new robe, 'the robe of righteousness', as a sign that the child has become a new person.

To remind them of their baptism, Orthodox Christians usually wear a small cross round their necks all the rest of their lives.

Chrismation

This word means 'anointing' or confirmation, and it follows immediately after the act of baptism. After a prayer, the priest anoints the child with chrism, or holy oil. He makes the sign of the cross on his brow, eyes, nostrils, lips, ears, chest, hands and feet. All the time the priest repeats the phrase: *'The seal of the gift of the Holy Spirit. Amen.'*

First Communion

The ceremony usually ends with the newly baptized and confirmed child being given his first communion.

The Roman Catholic Church

Baptism

In the Roman Catholic Church it is the custom to baptize children as soon as possible after birth.

The ceremony begins with the priest welcoming the parents, godparents, and the child at the church door. In the sacrament of baptism the priest's first questions are to make sure that the parents and godparents wish to bring up the child in the Christian way: *'loving God and our neighbour'*. After that promise the priest traces the sign of the cross on the child's forehead. He offers a prayer to ask God to give the child *'new life in abundance'*. This is followed by the blessing of the water for its holy use in baptism.

The parents and godparents promise to reject evil and profess their faith.

The priest then performs the baptism by pouring water on the child's head three times as he repeats the words:

'(Child's name), I baptize you in the name of the Father, and of the Son and of the Holy Spirit.'

The child is then anointed on the crown of his head with the holy oil.

As an outward sign of the Christian life the child is dressed in a white robe. A candle is lit for the child from the Paschal candle and the parents and godparents are told to help him *'to walk always as a child of the light'*.

The service ends in front of the altar, where a blessing is given to the parents and to the whole congregation.

First Communion

In the Roman Catholic tradition, children are admitted to Holy Communion before they are confirmed. They usually start receiving communion about the age of seven.

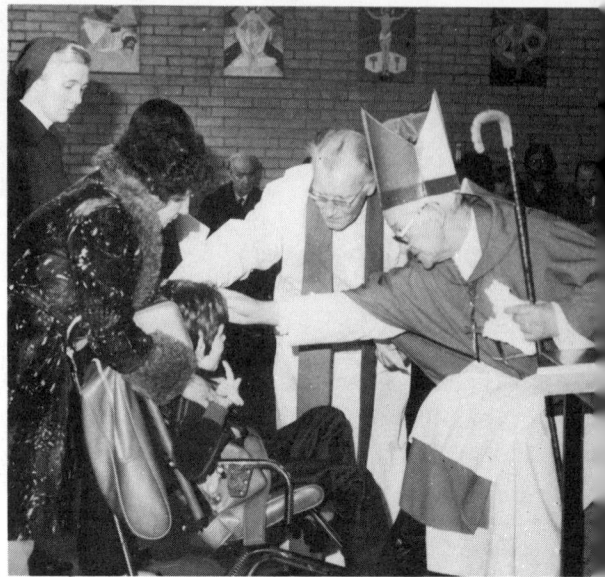

The thrill of receiving First Communion from their Bishop   A young disabled boy is confirmed

Confirmation

Confirmation takes place when the boy or girl is about twelve years old. At baptism the child has received his spiritual birth, and now, at confirmation, he gains spiritual strength. Candidates for confirmation have first of all to renew publicly the promises made for them at their baptism by parents and godparents.

The candidates and their sponsors form up in front of the bishop who performs the ceremony. He places his hand on the head of each person who is to be confirmed, anoints his forehead with the holy oil in the sign of the cross, and recites the words:

'(Name), be sealed with the Gift of the Holy Spirit'.

It is the custom for a Roman Catholic to adopt the name of a saint when he or she is confirmed. This gives them an example to inspire them and to live up to.

The Church of Scotland

Baptism

As in the Orthodox and Roman Catholic traditions, baptism in the Church of Scotland usually takes place during a Sunday service of worship. The words and acts of the service emphasize the responsibility of the whole Church for the children who are brought to the sacrament of baptism.

The babies are brought into the church by their parents during the singing of an appropriate hymn.

The minister stands at the font and reads some verses from the Bible about the importance of baptism. He reminds the parents that this sacrament is *'the appointed way of entrance into Christ's Church'*. He asks the parents to confess their faith and to promise to *'teach this child the truths and duties of the Christian faith, and by prayer and example to bring him (her) up in the life and worship of the Church'*.

The congregation are asked to stand as a sign that they also accept responsibility for helping the child to grow up *'in the knowledge and love of Christ'*.

Everyone confesses the faith in the words of the Apostles' Creed. Then the minister calls the people to prayer, and asks God to bless the water.

It is usually the father who brings the child to the font and tells the minister the Christian name. The minister takes the child in his arms, calls him by his Christian name or names, and sprinkles water on his head, saying:

'(Name), I baptize you in the name of the Father, and of the Son and of the Holy Spirit. AMEN.
The blessing of God Almighty, Father, Son, and Holy Spirit, descend upon you, and dwell in your heart for ever. AMEN.'

The congregation join in singing a blessing:

'The Lord bless you and keep you; the Lord make
his face to shine upon you, and be gracious unto
you; the Lord lift up his countenance upon
you, and give you peace. AMEN.'

The minister then states that the child *'is now received into the membership of the one, holy, catholic and apostolic Church'*.

The sacrament of baptism ends with further prayers, a hymn, and the final blessing.

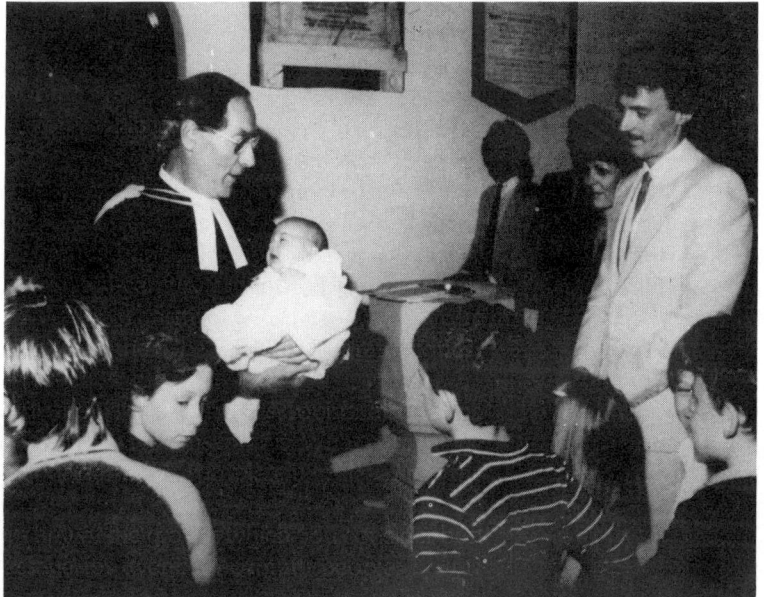

A Church of Scotland baptism in Bermuda

Confirmation

A Christian is a member of the Church from his baptism. The act of confirmation in the Church of Scotland means that a person comes to make a personal confession of the faith in which he or she has been brought up. This normally takes place when he or she is a teenager or young adult and able to think things out.

As in the Roman Catholic Church, the young person receives instruction about the Christian faith before the confirmation service. During the ceremony itself the young people stand in front of the congregation.

The minister reminds them of their baptism and asks them to 'confirm' by their own choice what was done on their behalf in childhood by their parents. Among the promises they are asked to make are these:

'To join regularly with your fellow Christians in worship.
'To be faithful in reading the Bible and in prayer.
'To give a fitting proportion of your time, talents and money for the Church's work in the world.'

The congregation stands while the candidates kneel. The minister lays his hand on the head of each, gives each one a blessing and prays that he may be strengthened in his faith. He admits the newly confirmed members 'to the fellowship of the Lord's Table'. Along with the elders, the minister shakes each of them by the hand as a sign of welcome and friendship.

The confirmation concludes with the saying of the Apostles' Creed and prayers.

First Communion

In the Church of Scotland, a person is admitted to his first communion by the act of confirmation. In recent years, however, there has been a great deal of discussion whether or not communion should be open to young children before they have been confirmed.

The Apostles' Creed

The Apostles' Creed which we find in the Church of Scotland service is an ancient Creed of the Church traditionally used in the West during the Baptismal Service. The words are:

I believe in God the Father Almighty, Maker of heaven and earth: And in Jesus Christ His only Son our Lord, Who was conceived by the Holy Ghost, Born of the Virgin Mary, Suffered under Pontius Pilate, Was crucified, dead, and buried, He descended into hell; The third day He rose again from the dead, He ascended into heaven, And sitteth on the right hand of God the Father Almighty; From thence He shall come to judge the quick and the dead.
I believe in the Holy Ghost; The holy Catholic Church; The Communion of Saints; The forgiveness of sins; The resurrection of the body; And the Life everlasting. AMEN.'

TEST YOUR UNDERSTANDING

- Old clothes and new clothes, facing West and facing East, white robes and lit candles, water and oil are all to be found within the Orthodox baptism service. Explain the significance of each of these.
- Describe the symbolic action in the Roman Catholic confirmation service through which the young person receives 'God's love and strength'.
- In the Church of Scotland the emphasis in confirmation is on the promises made by the young person. Copy out the promises under the headings: Public Worship; Private Worship; Service.
- Suggest a variety of ways in which a young person can give 'time, talents and money' for the work of the Church.

An Orthodox wedding ceremony

Marriage

All branches of the Church are agreed about the importance of marriage. In the Orthodox and Roman Catholic traditions marriage is one of the sacraments.

The Orthodox Church

According to the teaching of the Orthodox Church, God does not intend that man should live alone, but as a member of a family. Just as the Bible tells that God blessed the first couple, Adam and Eve, so the Church continues to bless marrying couples today.

The Orthodox marriage ceremony is divided into two parts which used to take place on separate occasions, but which now form one celebration.

The first part of the ceremony is known as Betrothal. This is held in the entrance to the church building. The man and woman make their marriage promises, and rings are blessed and exchanged. The exchange of rings is an outward sign that the two partners are joining together in marriage freely and willingly.

The priest then leads the couple in procession to the centre of the church and they stand in front of a small table containing a copy of the Gospels and a cross. The couple hold lighted candles as a sign of their common faith in Christ, the Light of the World.

The second part of the ceremony is known as the Crowning. It begins with prayers and reaches a climax with the placing of gold or silver crowns or wreaths of flowers and leaves on the heads of the couple. They are crowned as king and queen of a family.

The priest recites the words: '*O Lord God, crown them with glory and honour*'. The crowns are symbols of joy, but they also stand for martyrdom, reminding the couple that they are to be witnesses to Christ in the world. Every family, in fact, is regarded as a small image or picture of the Kingdom of God.

The priest then reads from the Bible to remind those present of the duties and responsibilities of family life and of the importance Jesus placed on marriage.

After further prayers, the priest presents a cup of wine to the couple. In sharing the same cup and drinking from it, they show that they will share each other's lives.

The service ends with the bride and bridegroom joining hands and being led by the priest three times round the table. By walking in a circle they are showing that their marriage, like a circle, has no end, and is intended to last for ever. As he leads them round the table, the priest carries a cross to point out the way in which all Christians must walk.

The Roman Catholic Church

Within the Roman Catholic tradition, marriage usually takes place during Mass. The homily which is given in the Liturgy of the Word stresses the importance of Christian marriage and the responsibilities of the couple in bringing up their children.

Then there follows the Liturgy of Marriage. It begins with the priest reminding the bride and bridegroom that they have come to church so that *'the Lord may seal and strengthen your love'*.

The couple are asked if they:

undertake the obligations of marriage freely and deliberately;

will be faithful to each other for the rest of their lives;

will accept children lovingly from God and bring them up within the Church.

The couple then declare their willingness to take each other as husband and wife and the marriage promises are made with them holding each other by the right hand:

'I . . .
take you . . .
for my lawful wife/husband
to have and to hold
from this day forward;
for better, for worse;
for richer, for poorer;
in sickness and in health
till death do us part.'

The ring or rings are blessed by the priest and are given as a sign of the couple's love and faith in each other.

Then follows the Liturgy of the Eucharist, during which the Nuptial Blessing is given. This ends with words such as the following:

'Father,
keep them always true to your commandments
keep them faithful in marriage
and let them be living examples of Christian life.
Give them the strength which comes from the Gospel
so that they may be witnesses of Christ to others.
Bless them with children
and help them to be good parents.

This is followed by Holy Communion, through which the couple's love is strengthened and they are brought closer to Christ and to each other.

The Church of Scotland

The minister usually leads the bride into the church where she joins the bridegroom in front of the communion table. In the opening words of the service, everyone present is reminded of the purpose of Christian marriage:

> *'Lifelong companionship, comfort and joy between husband and wife.*
> *The right and proper setting for the full expression of physical love between man and woman.*
> *The ordering of family life, where children — who are also God's gifts to us — may enjoy the security of love and the heritage of faith.*
> *The well-being of human society, which can be stable and happy only when the marriage bond is honoured and upheld.'*

The minister then asks if there is any reason why the couple may not lawfully be married to each other. This is followed by a prayer in which God's blessing is asked on the marriage.

The marriage vows are made while the man and woman hold each other by the right hand:

> *'I . . ., now take you, . . . to be my wife/husband. In the presence of God and before these witnesses I promise to be a loving, faithful and loyal husband/wife to you, until God shall separate us by death'.*

A Church of Scotland
marriage ceremony

This is followed by the exchange of a ring, or rings, and the minister says:

'By this sign you take each other, to have and to hold from this day forward, for better, for worse; for richer, for poorer; in sickness and in health; to love and to cherish, till death do you part.'

The minister then declares them to be husband and wife:

'In the name of the Father, and of the Son, and of the Holy Spirit'.

The service ends with a blessing, a Bible reading, a prayer, and the Benediction.

TEST YOUR UNDERSTANDING

- Lighted candles, crowns or wreaths, a cup of wine, a cross, and walking in a circle are all features of the Orthodox Church marriage ceremony. Explain what each of these represents.
- Study the Roman Catholic and Church of Scotland outlines of the marriage service. Pay particular attention to:
    the marriage promises;
    the Nuptial Blessing (in the Roman Catholic service);
    the purpose of Christian marriage (stated in the Church of Scotland service).
  Put forward an argument for or against the Christian idea of marriage in the light of today's rapidly changing society.

Death

The Orthodox Church

When an Orthodox Christian dies, his body is washed and then dressed in new clothes as an outward sign of the new life which Christians look for beyond the grave. Psalms and prayers for the dead are read over the body.

A strip of material containing pictures of Jesus, Mary his mother and John the Baptist is placed on the forehead. This represents the victory wreath of an athlete who has successfully run his race. A picture of Jesus is placed on the hands as a sign that the person believed in Jesus and gave his life to him. Then the body is covered with a special cloth as a sign of the protection given by Jesus.

At the funeral, four candlesticks are placed at the sides of the coffin to form a cross. The mourners hold lighted candles as a sign that the dead person's life has not been extinguished.

During the Orthodox funeral service, everyone present is made to face up to the basic questions of life and death. At the last, do they see tragedy or victory, death or resurrection?

The deceased lies in the centre of the church, facing the altar. The coffin is usually open so that the body is in full view. Thus everyone present is brought face to face with the fact of death, 'the final enemy'. But that is only one side of the

Russian and Armenian graves at the
Russian cemetery of Sainte
Geneviève-des-Bois, Paris

picture. Having faced death, the mourners are better able to appreciate the miracle of new life brought about by Christ's resurrection. Everything about the service points to that.

The order of service reminds everyone of Sunday worship, which is the weekly celebration of the day Jesus rose from the dead. The priest wears white vestments. The church is full of lights. There are burning candles and incense, symbols of life and prayer. The Bible readings emphasize eternal life and the resurrection of Christ. Everything in the service is an outward sign that:

'*Christ is risen from the dead*
trampling down death by death
and upon those in the tombs bestowing life'

The Roman Catholic Church

There are three main divisions or 'stations' within the funeral rite of the Roman Catholic Church.

The first of these takes place at the dead person's home or at the hospital where he died. Prayers are said before the body is taken to the church.

The second station takes place at the church. Usually the body is brought to the church the evening before the funeral Mass is to be celebrated. The priest receives the relatives of the dead person at the door of the church and sprinkles the body with holy water. The coffin is normally placed in front of the altar. After the priest has offered words of greeting and sympathy to the relatives he says prayers. The Gospel or a Bible or a cross may be placed on the coffin. The Paschal candle is placed at the head of the coffin as a symbol of the Easter mystery of new life and a sign of Christian hope in the resurrection.

In recent years there have been changes in the funeral Mass. The central theme now is the resurrection of Christ. As a reminder of this the priest usually wears white vestments. The emphasis is not on fear or grief or loss but on God's faithfulness and the Christian hope. At the same time the Mass keeps the solemn atmosphere of awe which all people feel when they face the mystery of death.

After the Mass comes the final commendation and farewell. This begins with an invitation to prayer. The priest sprinkles the body with holy water and uses incense. The holy water is a reminder of the person's entry into eternal life through the water of baptism. The incense is a sign that the body is the temple of the Holy Spirit.

There follow prayers and chants and the body is taken from the church to the sound of words such as:

'I am the resurrection and the life;
He who believes in me, even if he is dead, shall live;
and all who live and believe in me, will never die.'

The third station takes place at the graveside, where the rite is short and simple. Usually the grave has already been blessed; if not, it is blessed before the burial. As the body is lowered into the grave the priest says:

It has pleased Almighty God to call our brother from this life to Himself. Accordingly we commit his body to the earth whence it came. Since Christ, the first fruits of the dead, has risen again and will refashion our frail body in the pattern of his glorious risen body, we commend our brother to the Lord. May he embrace him in his peace and bring his body to life again on the last day.'

This is followed by prayers which usually include the words:

'Eternal rest grant to him (her) O Lord,
And let perpetual light shine upon him (her).'

A service of cremation occasionally takes the place of burial.

The Bishop officiates at the graveside of the funeral of a parish priest

The Church of Scotland

The Book of Common Order of the Church of Scotland provides for two services: one at the dead person's home or in a church, the other at the graveside or at the crematorium. When a cremation takes place there is often just a single service in the crematorium chapel.

The minister begins the service with the words:

'Let us worship God'.

After a Psalm or Hymn, the minister reminds the people of comforting words from the Bible, such as:

'Blessed are those who mourn, for they shall be comforted.
The eternal God is your dwelling place, and underneath are the everlasting arms.
The souls of the righteous are in the hand of God, and no torment will ever touch them. They are at peace.'

There follow prayers and readings from the Bible and a short talk to remind the mourners of their Christian hope.

Then the minister says further prayers with such words as:

'Ever blessed God . . . we praise thee for all who on earth fought a good fight, finished their course and kept the faith, and are now at rest in thee. We remember with gratitude our loved ones whom thou hast called hence, especially thy servant (name). We thank thee for all thy loving kindness towards him (her) which upheld him (her) in sickness and in health, in joy and in sorrow. We praise thee for all that he (she) was by nature and by grace. We bless thee for the good which thou didst enable him (her) to do and for the memories he (she) has left behind.
'Now trusting in thine infinite mercy, we commend him (her) to thee.
'Rest eternal grant unto him (her), O Lord,
And let light perpetual shine upon him (her).'

At the grave, the minister says:

'We have entrusted our brother/sister (name) into the hands of God, and we now commit his (her) body to the ground, earth to earth, ashes to ashes, dust to dust; having our whole trust and confidence in the mercy of our heavenly Father, and in the victory of his Son, Jesus Christ our Lord, who died, was buried, and rose again for us, and is alive and reigns for ever and ever. AMEN.'

Similar words are spoken at a crematorium service.

The service ends with such words as:

'Blessed are the dead which die in the Lord from henceforth:
yea, saith the Spirit, that they may rest from their labours and their works do follow them.

The minister says short prayers and finally blesses the people with the Benediction.

In this modern crematorium the coffin is placed in the walled enclosure at the far corner and is lowered out of view at the moment of committal

TEST YOUR UNDERSTANDING

- The outward acts which surround the death and funeral of an Orthodox Christian have inner meanings. Comment on the significance of each of the following:

  dressing the body in new clothes;

  placing a strip of material on the forehead of the dead person;

  placing a picture of Jesus on the hands of the dead person;

  covering the body with a special cloth;

  placing the open coffin in the centre of the church;

  the priest wearing white vestments;

  burning of candles and sprinkling of incense.
- The Roman Catholic services also make use of outward actions to show beliefs and hopes. Try to explain the significance of each of the following which all take place within the church:

  placing the Gospel book or Bible or cross on the coffin;

  placing the Paschal candle at the head of the coffin;

  sprinkling the body with holy water and incense.
- Study the prayer which is quoted in the Church of Scotland service. State in your own words all the things God is being thanked and praised for.

MAKING A NEW WORLD: PART 2

Jesus' world was a world of fishermen and farmers, tax-collectors and Roman soldiers, of sword and spear. Jesus travelled on foot and spread his message by word of mouth. The 20th century is a world of computer experts and mass unemployment, of super powers and nuclear missiles, of jet travel and the mass media. What have the life and the teaching of Jesus to do with the issues and concerns of the 20th century?

In the introduction to Luke's Gospel, we said that Luke was concerned to show that God was at work through Jesus in bringing about a new world. In this chapter we will be looking for evidence that the process of building this new world is continuing. As man's knowledge and understanding grow in our rapidly changing world, so the Church's insights and activities develop and change. New answers are offered to old questions, new questions and challenges are introduced by science and technology.

Making a New World – At Home

The following articles and reports from newspapers and Church publications show some of the things which Christians do as individuals or in groups. Working at times with people who hold different beliefs, they share a concern for bringing about a better way of life for all in their community.

SHORT BACK AND SIDES – PLEASE! Haircut marathon in aid of Yorkhill

Sunday was a cut above the average for Maureen Crolla ... she shampooed, cut and blow-dried the hair of 200 people in 11 hours – and for no charge.

With the help of three colleagues Maureen hopes to have raised around £2000 from sponsor money and donations for the bone marrow transplant, cancer research and brain-scan units of Glasgow's Yorkhill Hospital.

'I got the idea after watching a television programme about bone marrow transplant operations,' says Maureen. 'Children are dying because there is not enough money to pay for the operations.'

She decided to do what she could to help.

A day to think about being a good neighbour

Theme is: Caring with your eyes open

'CARING with your eyes open' is the theme of Social Responsibility Sunday today.

'Social responsibility means caring – caring about the elderly person next door who might need someone to drop in every now and then; caring about the sick, the old, the disabled and the lonely.'

With nearly 1200 staff and hundreds of committed volunteers the Kirk's work in helping people is a mammoth and professional task.

The Church of Scotland's work for the needy goes beyond providing basic services. Its work is done in a pioneering spirit and it is always looking at ways to improve services and meet the changing demands of society.

For example, the Kirk is soon to open a new home in Glasgow to care for the 'confused elderly.' So far there are no other homes in Scotland for older people who are mentally frail, many of whom are either in existing homes or in hospital. At the moment some of these older people are in hospital unnecessarily because there is nowhere else for them to go.

The new home is Williamwood House. It will cater for about 25 older people.

Growing problem

The Church of Scotland's social services change according to new needs. For example, some of its children's homes are closing because of the regional council's policy of promoting fostering and adoption.

The officer-in-charge helps a resident to read a large-print Bible

These homes will not lie empty. The Kirk is already considering ways of using them. Two possibilities are to provide care for mentally-handicapped adults or for people put on probation by the courts.

Homelessness and rootlessness among single men and women is a growing problem in the cities. Many are down-and-outs, some are alcoholics, and some are simply in need of shelter.

The Church's night shelter in Glasgow, Kirkhaven, offers a place to go during the day, friends to meet, someone to talk to, a cup of tea and lots of creative activities. At night it serves as a shelter for the totally homeless and is always about 99% full.

Chaplain on march to save his parish

The Number One blast furnace at Ravenscraig has more in common with Hell than Heaven, but this is the heart of the Rev. John Potter's parish. As a glowing river of molten iron gushes and cascades through smoke and flame below him, he edges along a narrow catwalk to spread the Gospel.

Mr Potter is industrial chaplain at the huge Lanarkshire steel plant, and as the jobs of the 5000 workforce come under increasing threat, he has become more and more involved in their struggle to survive.

Scotland has 92 such chaplains, clergymen of all denominations, who work in factories, shipyards and industrial estates. However, closures, redundancies and spiralling unemployment are prompting the churchmen into forms of direct action which might have been deemed unseemly a decade ago.

Last week Mr Potter, a mild-mannered Methodist, travelled with a delegation to London to raise support for the Ravenscraig cause. He marched alongside demonstrators and took his place on the same speakers' platform as Michael Foot and Mick McGahey.

It was perhaps dangerously close to a demonstration of political, rather than pastoral, concern.

'It was a risky thing to do,' he concedes, 'both for me personally and for the Church but I considered it more risky not to go. Then the Ravenscraig men could have said – when it came to the crunch, where were you?'

THE KIDS WITH FAITH
IN THE FUTURE *St Columba's show the way*

The Good News is being proclaimed by the pupils of St Columba's High School, Clydebank.

The practical Christian response of the school is characterised by the range of activities in which the pupils so enthusiastically participate.

The pupils are quick to focus on the needs of those in their immediate environment.

This was seen earlier on in the school year when pupils made and delivered personal invitations to the elderly of the community. Entertaining them to a meal and afterwards to a concert.

While the efforts of staff and pupils to raise money and send clothes to Mother Teresa of Calcutta demonstrates the fact that St Columba's is not wholly inward looking, but is also aware of the needs of the wider Christian Community.

More recently first and second year pupils raised the sum of £72 from their Christmas dance and purchased a slide projector which will be presented to The Little Sisters of the Poor, of St Joseph's Convent, Greenock.

If a society is to be judged by the way it treats its weakest and most vulnerable members, St Columba's is certainly forging positively ahead with its Pro-life Cell.

The cell, which was established three years ago, consists of pupils from S3-S6. The aim of the cell is to offer mothers an alternative to abortion by providing material aid.

Over the past three years six babies have been 'adopted' by the school through the proceeds of ventures launched with the school's support. While the parents of the pupils readily offer baby clothes, prams and cots which are passed on to the Innocents.

No Christian community is complete without its spiritual dimension and St Columba's Charismatic Renewal Group serves to function as a 'way-station'.

It serves the school and the wider community by prayer and intercession, and providing opportunities for pupils who feel the need for a deepening of faith – a closer encounter.

The values and accepted standards of today's society are not always desirable, especially if we claim to be living by the precepts of Christianity.

The Justice and Peace Group in St Columba's sets out to question and to take many of these values to task.

The group is affiliated to Amnesty International, Campaign Against the Arms Trade, Pax Christi, Aid to the Church in Need and the Campaign for Nuclear Disarmament.

The Group participates in demonstrations for 'life issues' such as nuclear weapons and abortion. It also participates in the Amnesty Letter Writing Campaign.

One of the ambitious ventures undertaken in St Columba's has been its Lourdes Handicapped Project. (The Project began during the school session 1979/80 with St Columba's High School sixth year pupils.)

During that summer mainly through the profits of the Tuck Shop, St Columba's raised enough money to send five mentally handicapped young persons plus their parents to Lourdes.

A HAVEN OF PEACE ...
AND A PLACE OF REST

PEACE... perfect peace is the gift of Christ.

And that is the mission of the Sisters of Charity.

They bring that peace to the sick and the dying in their hospice, St Margaret's.

The friendly Irish nuns, headed by Sister Josepha, are charming, kind and caring.

'Gloom,' said Sister Josepha, 'is not something you will find around here.'

'It's a special kind of nursing home. It is free from general hospital pressures, surgery theatres, laboratories and so on and the staff have more time to attend to the needs of the patients.'

As well as in-patient treatment, St Margaret's provides day care services to allow patients to stay at home and to receive nursing and medical care as an out-patient.

The Sisters do home visits – 'To support families and to give them the confidence they need to look after their loved ones at home.'

'Then we have "sitter services" which consist of volunteers who will sit with a patient at home for an hour or two,

perhaps reading to the patient or playing a game with them.'

The aims of all these services, say the Sisters, is to enable patients to live as full a life as possible in the time that remains to them.

The hospice is open to all, no matter what their age, race, class or creed.

Making   New World – Abroad

For centuries the Church in the West has sent missionaries and money to other parts of the world. More recently, the pattern has been one of partnership, working with churches in the Third World and learning from them how help can best be given. Today things have turned full circle. The Church in the West has come to realize that as well as being able to help others, it also has a great deal to learn from Christians in other parts of the world.

The first six articles in this section tell us how Christians from the West are helping others in different parts of the world. Then come three articles about the situation in South Africa. The first of these is a report on the stance taken by the South African Council of Churches. The other two show how Christians in Britain are responding to the call for help from the South African Churches. Then come two reports about how Christians from the Third World are sharing their faith with British Christians.

Many of the concerns of the Church today are highlighted by the situation in El Salvador. So we finish this chapter with a case study of the Church in El Salvador where Christians are trying to work for a just and fair life in a situation of persecution and a great deal of suffering.

Picture this . . .

Since before Christmas, the porch of Motherwell's Cathedral has been graced by a portrait of Mother Teresa, painted by Newarthill amateur artist Mrs Nora Sharkey.

So far the Cathedral's third world projects – providing medicines for Uganda and assisting a school building project in Kouve, Togoland – have benefitted by more than £1000 from money gathered in the collection box placed beneath the picture.

DIET OF RICE AND WATER . . .

A bowl of rice and a glass of water is the diet of many in the Third World – and also lunch for some at St Cuthbert's High School, Johnstone.

Senior Pupils and Staff have been giving up their lunch money to the Save the Children Fund's Ethiopia Appeal, in return for rice and water.

The picture shows some of the participants getting into the spirit of things, and engaging at the same time in two of the oldest Lenten practices – Fasting and Almsgiving.

I'M GOING TO BE A FOOTBALLER

Five-year-old Mohammed fractured his femur when he fell down the steep, muddy terrace outside his home in Baglung, Nepal, and he arrived at our clinic with his leg swollen, painful – and shortened.

Normal traction was going to be impossible. We didn't have the equipment and there was no bed at home. Our team decided to use a Thomas splint – a long metal contraption that would lengthen Mohammed's leg and keep the healing bone straight. They persuaded the local blacksmith to make one, and explained to his parents about the careful nursing he would need.

Staff paid regular home visits and when the splint came off after six weeks Mohammed's leg had healed well. Soon he was playing his beloved football. Without the resourcefulness of the SCF team Mohammed could have been severely crippled for life.

From prison cell to Blantyre

Prisoner of Conscience Mrs Purificacion Trinidad of the Philippines has managed to reply to a letter sent by an Observer reader in Blantyre following a story in the issue of January 7, which highlighted her plight.

Amnesty International in Scotland adopted Purificacion and her husband Rolieto as prisoners of conscience following their arrest for 'violation of the anti-subversion law'. They had a human rights meeting in their house.

The message reads:

'Thank you for your greetings sent on our detention. I assure you it has given me the needed strength and hope in these trying months.

'My husband, housed in separate quarters and kept padlocked, joins me in thanking you.

'Let this small card I made in my cell be a sincere expression of appreciation and solidarity.'

A MATTER OF WORLD CONSCIENCE – GOSPEL ACTION

'Such a battle ... so great a victory'

Leprosy is still the most feared and terrible affliction man must endure.

This Sunday is World Leprosy Sunday, when people throughout Britain will be asked to donate what they can towards the alleviation of the disease.

Prayers for this work are vitally important, both for the sufferers of leprosy and the people who work at breaking down the barriers and segregation.

Jesus Himself showed His mercy and kindness when He cured the leper.

To care for the leper is a Gospel action, following in the footsteps of Christ.

The dedication of the people who work with lepers is recalled by Fr. Pallottini who worked with them in Ethiopia.

'A few miles from the centre of Addis Ababa, there is a leprosy village, swarming with lepers, and always in attendance upon them a small army of doctors, supervisors, nurses and auxiliaries.

'Believe me, I have never known an army as small as this one fight such a battle and win so great a victory.

'I battled with them against this ter-rifying disease, never losing my admiration for their courage and their dedication.'

Missionaries like Fr. Pallottini are working in Asia, Africa and South America where the terrible disease of leprosy is still causing havoc.

Fr. Pallottini always stresses the difficulty they find in breaking down the barriers and isolation lepers suffer and creating an atmosphere where lepers are accepted and not shunned. 'You must understand that the leprosy patient suffers less from his disease than from his segregation.'

Although the problems of leprosy are still great today, it is encouraging to see the progress which has been made by comparing conditions now with Fr. Pallottini's accounts of the start of his work in Ethiopia 12 years ago.

'When I started my leprosy work in Ethiopia in 1970, we were forbidden to say that leprosy existed in that country when thousands of them were roaming around the towns and villages and even the capital.

'And there were many more banished to deserted and abandoned places, hiding in derelict cemeteries, or maybe even worse, interned in camps behind barbed wire fences, with machine guns trained on them by armed guards – an unimaginable world of horror, pain and despair.'

Fr. Pallottini says: 'It took a long time to change the attitude of the government, to secure the freedom of these poor people, to get protection and medical treatment for them, and finally by building clinics near their own villages, giving the chance to be reunited with their own families.'

'It was just as difficult to change the attitude of the lepers themselves. When we opened the gates of their camps we were literally assaulted. With the memories of those camps still vivid in them, small wonder that they had lost faith in all men.'

Compare these pictures of his early work with the scenes when patients he worked with came back to see him, often bringing their children, and thanking him for the love and care he gave them.

THE DONS IN AFRICA

The Rev. Bob Bone is chaplain at Livingstonia Secondary School, in the north of Malawi. An unusual, but very productive area of partnership is in the work he does with the football team. The team takes the field in an Aberdeen Football Club strip – a present from manager Alex Ferguson and the club. They train every weekday morning at 5.15 a.m.! Hard work and long journeys had taken them to the semi-finals of the Northern Regions schools' tournament. The fellowship which has been built up has been tremendous. Their conduct on and off the field has been admired.

MIXED RACES

The mainly 'white' Presbyterian Church of Southern Africa took a courageous stand at its General Assembly when it called on its ministers to defy the Mixed Marriages Act and marry people irrespective of race. The Assembly also urged its ministers, when preaching, to disregard restrictions which prevent them from quoting banned people or publications. In addition it invited congregations to protest peacefully against apartheid.

The Government has continued to harass trade union leaders, ministers and students opposed to apartheid through detentions and house searches. The South African Council of Churches was again the subject of innuendos and rumours regarding its financial affairs. (It supports the families of political prisoners and those who suffer hardship in the 'removals'.)

Writing to Churches in Europe and the U.S.A. in November 1981, Bishop Tutu, the General Secretary of the South African Council of Churches, said:

'We continue to call on the international community to help us by exerting pressure (political, diplomatic and above all, economic) to persuade the South African Government to come to the conference table before it is too late.

There is no real change in South Africa. International hotels, mixed sport, etc., are merely cosmetic and superficial. Real change has to do with political powersharing. We have said if the Government did only four things as the beginning to change, we would tell our people. "Be patient, they are now talking about real change". They must (a) have one citizenship for all South Africans in an undivided South Africa; (b) abolish the Pass Laws even if it is phased to avoid chaos; (c) stop immediately the vicious policy of population removal and (d) establish a uniform education system.

We talk peaceful change and we are vilified. Soon blacks will get disillusioned and embittered and then we will have the bloodbath which could start World War III.'

South African Fruit Boycott

The Church of Scotland Woman's Guild has urged all its members to boycott South African fruit and other goods in protest against the system of apartheid.

A leaflet was sent to all Guild branches urging them, 'support the fight for justice in South Africa – do not buy South African fruit.'

The leaflet depicts the fruits of apartheid as detention without trial, forced removals, poverty and violence and quotes Bishop Desmond Tutu, Chairman of the South African Council of Churches, as saying: 'Boycotts are one of the few ways left to bring change peacefully.'

'The Church of Scotland Woman's Guild calls upon its members to refrain from buying South African products,' says the leaflet. 'Apartheid is a racist policy which denies black South Africans basic human rights.'

'The South African Council of Churches has called on Christians around the world to exert economic pressure on South Africa. One of the ways we can do this is by boycotting South African goods like fresh and tinned fruit.'

It quotes John Vorster, ex-Prime Minister of South Africa, as saying that every time South African goods are bought it means a new brick in the wall of the continued existence of the present system and asks if Guild and other church members are prepared to continue to build the wall of apartheid.

The leaflet states that black South Africans, who comprise 80% of the population, are only given 13% of the land. Two million blacks have been forcibly removed and another two million are due for removal.

'Removal usually means uprooting black families from "white" areas and dumping them in remote and desolate areas with a tent and a corrugated iron toilet. They start life again with no schools, no proper water supply, no cultivated land and no jobs,' it says.

The Kirk workers who face violence

When the General Assembly of the Church of Scotland endorses a list of human rights recommendations later this week, it will affect the lives of some of its most devoted members: the missionaries and church workers abroad.

For them, death threats and violence are occupational hazards. Life has long been difficult and often dangerous for those who spread the Gospel worldwide, and, the Assembly will learn, is no less so today.

The Assembly will be asked to protest to the South African Government over the forced removal of black communities from their traditional homes in the Mgwali region. It will also be asked to call on all its congregations to support a boycott of South African imported goods.

The Church of Scotland's anti-apartheid stance has already brought reprisals. Some of the 5000 blacks to be moved from Mgwali live on land acquired by the Church 120 years ago. Church offices have been raided recently by South African special branch agents, and three Church officials have had their homes searched.

FAITH SHARING
The Global Dimension of the Church

Congregations from Jedburgh to Aberdeen received a visit from three overseas church representatives between September and November in the sixth of the 'Operation Faithshare' scheme tours since 1972.

The trio accepted the invitation to tour 12 Presbyteries throughout Scotland as part of the programme designed to emphasise the worldwide character of the Christian church. They were Rev. Noel S. Sen, chaplain to the Bishop of Calcutta, Registrar of the Diocese and a member of the Synod of the Church of North India, a member church of the Anglican Communion.

From Jamaica came Miss Verna Cassells, Youth Director and a deaconess with the United Church of Jamaica and Grand Cayman.

The third visitor, Mr Duncan C. Kangulu, is an elder in the Blantyre Synod of the Church of Central Africa Presbyterian.

They shared their faith and experience with groups and congregations in churches up and down the country, and brought the greetings of the churches in their own countries.

The trio were asked at the end of their visit to outline their impressions and experience of Scotland and her churches.

They were emphatic that the Church of Scotland should do more to meet the needs of young people.

Nigerian Christians
(written by a former missionary)

Nigerian Christians can help us to see ourselves as others see us, to re-examine our attitudes to the amount of money we spend on arms, and on aid, our attitude to the South African Government and to our own life-style. Some years ago a Nigerian Anglican wrote 'already we say to Nigerians visiting Britain, that they go as Christians to a largely pagan country and if they receive offence as many do at one time or another, to remember that they are not going there to receive the Gospel but to take it, and not to requite offence with offence but to show a better way'.

The name of El Salvador today brings pictures of ever increasing violence and terror. During 1982 there were 6,007 documented cases of murder and disappearance.

Poverty and Politics

The majority of Salvadoreans have always been poor. Homes in the countryside are single rooms of mud and wattle, and in the city they are often makeshift efforts of cardboard and rubbish, without pure water, drainage or electricity. But there is also a small sector of extremely rich Salvadoreans, whose luxurious houses are surrounded by high walls and guarded by the army.

In the 1960s peasants and urban workers tried to organise into cooperatives, unions and political parties. The landowners however, supported by the army, resorted to brutal methods to keep their position. Leaders of such groups were assassinated, and it became dangerous to join any kind of opposition.

A military dictatorship was replaced in 1979 by a civilian-military junta which promised reforms, but the army's violence continued and made reforms impossible, so its civilian members resigned. Some actually joined the opposition.

A Campaign of Terror

The regular army of El Salvador together with special security forces like the National Guard, has been accused of mass killings. There are also unofficial forces of informers and 'death squads', which capture, torture and murder, and terrorise the countryside. The death squads are suspected of close cooperation with the official security forces.

The Human Rights Commission of El Salvador and the Catholic Legal Aid office have documented thousands of disappearances, and cases of mutilated bodies appearing daily in the street. Their evidence suggests that most of these deaths are the work of the security forces and death squads.

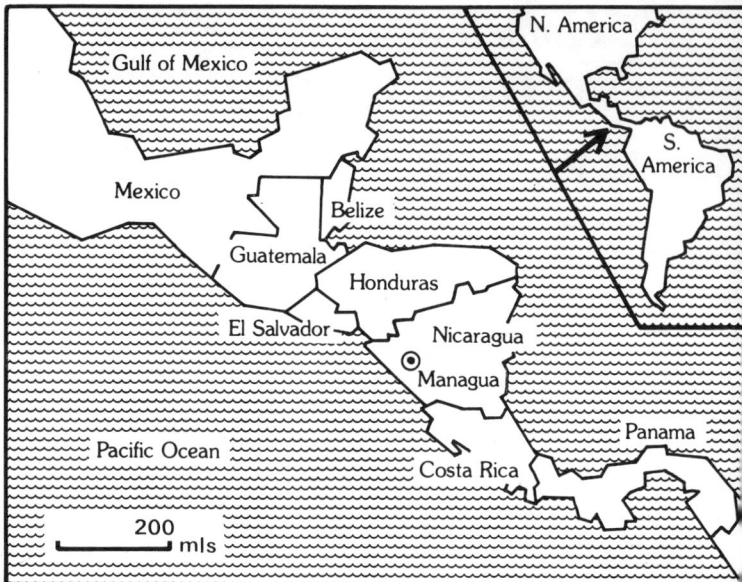

Deaths and Disappearances

1980	13,194 civilians killed
1981	13,553 civilians killed
Since March 1982	About 300 deaths per month

These are only the documented cases; many more clearly take place, especially in rural areas.

Particular Murders Include:

March 1980	Archbishop Romero
November 1980	6 FDR leaders
December 1980	4 US missionaries
September 1980	Jose Arcevido, a well known lay Christian teacher
March 1983	Marienella Garcia Villas, President, Human Rights Commission

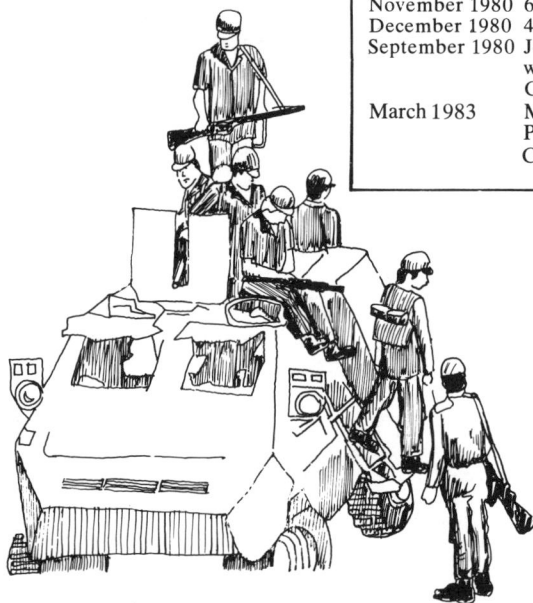

The Homeless

The 500,000 homeless people within El Salvador take refuge in camps often run by the church. The San Jose refuge, for example, in the garden of the Catholic Seminary, has 1,600 refugees; the people have built wooden shelters and organised health care and education for the children. But food is poor and scarce. Entering or leaving the camp is so dangerous that the inmates are virtually prisoners.

Camps in the countryside are desperate. There are huge numbers of people living in fear of the soldiers and unable to get enough food. In all the camps cases of malnutrition, dysentery, worms, lice and severe colds are common. Many water supplies are contaminated by dumped corpses.

Refugees, relief workers and priests are often accused by the army of being 'subversives' or 'communists', and are constantly harassed.

The Church in El Salvador

Many priests, nuns, lay Christian teachers and Christian communities have taken up the cause of the poor, but such people who had been teaching and helping people have often 'disappeared'.

The best known church leader was Archbishop Oscar Romero. Caring deeply about the suffering of his people, he courageously condemned the violence that kept most of them in poverty and hunger, and prevented them making their voice heard. As 'the voice of those who have no voice' he spoke up for them by sermons and radio and by appealing publicly to the army and to world leaders, and he set up schemes to relieve poverty.

Archbishop Romero was shot just before Holy Week 1980, while saying mass in San Salvador.

The work begun by Archbishop Romero for families of the 'disappeared', peasants forced off their land and victims of violence has been supported since 1978, but even this is now limited, and for the past three years most grants have been for emergency help for the homeless.

Christian Aid and El Salvador

Since 1980 £424,610 has been given for this work done by a church organisation of Catholics, Baptists and others, which runs nine refugee camps. The work is difficult; one member of staff disappeared in 1982 and another was forced into exile.

Real progress in fighting poverty will only be possible when there is peace, and a determination by those in power to allow the poor to improve their lives, and to encourage those who are helping them.

"I have frequently been threatened with death. I ought to say as a Christian, I do not believe in death without resurrection.... from this moment I offer my blood for the redemption and resurrection of El Salvador. May my death, if it is accepted by God, be for the liberation of my people and as a witness of hope in what is to come. Can you tell them, if they succeed in killing me, that I pardon and bless those who do it.. A bishop may die, but the church of God, which is the people, will never die".

Archbishop Oscar Romero

TEST YOUR UNDERSTANDING

- Having read the articles and reports in this chapter, list the different groups of people who are being helped by Christians today in this country and overseas.
- Christians are concerned with salvation or 'health'. From the articles you have read, what in your opinion are the greatest barriers to a full and healthy life? Give reasons for your answers.
- What problems are Christians tackling today which were not tackled by Jesus?
- Which of the articles do you think shows the most imaginative way of tackling a problem?

Making a New World – Difficult Decisions

The following extracts from *The Glasgow Herald* focus on two issues, both concerning the value of life, one from the world of personal relationships, the other from the national and international scene. The extracts show how Christians try to apply their religious beliefs to the contemporary world. Two short extracts on birth control are added to the passages on abortion to highlight the fact that there is a lively debate going on today within the main Christian traditions in Scotland on issues such as these.

Abortion

Extract 1

Kirk asked to act on abortion

A review of the 1967 Abortion Act is called for in the Church of Scotland's board of social responsibility report to the General Assembly, which opens next Saturday.

The Assembly will be asked to support the call for a review based on the findings of a study group, which claims the 1967 Act has led to abortion on demand. The report describes that situation as "an intolerable abdication of society's obligations to protect the weakest and most helpless members of the species."

The group recommends that the church should reaffirm the Biblical and historic Christian conviction in the sanctity of all human life. From the beginning, it argues, the foetus is an independent human being made in the image of God. It concludes from this conviction that the inviolability of the foetus can be threatened only in the case of risk to maternal life – after exhaustion of all alternatives.

The report also calls on the Church to consider ways in which alternatives to abortion can be put to those with difficult pregnancies, and how support may be provided for them through encouragement of voluntary agencies, counselling facilities, accommodation, and practical assistance.

It is not enough for the Church to condemn the widespread practice of abortion, says the report. Sympathetic and practical counselling should be available for those confronted with "the awful dilemma."

The Glasgow Herald 10/5/85

Extract 2

Kirk restricts its backing for abortion

A move to introduce much tighter restrictions on the conditions under which abortions may be carried out was narrowly approved yesterday by the Assembly.

It decided by a majority of forty votes to support the view of its Board of Social Responsibility that abortion should be acceptable only in cases where the mother's life is at risk.

The Glasgow Herald 23/5/85

Extract 4

ABORTION THE EASY OPTION

Sir, – The Church of Scotland's reversal of last year's stand in support of the unborn child not only disappoints but astounds me. Apparently last year's decision caused much "consternation" and according to the Herald editorial "put the Church in a bad light." I was not aware that public opinion shaped the moral and ethical code of the Church.

In the light of the conclusion reached by the Assembly study group "that the embryo was genetically complete from the moment of conception and had rights as a human being," it is surely impossible to advocate abortion under any circumstances.

Having established that the unborn child has "rights as a human being" we accord him/her equal status with the rest of society. Or are we to believe that there are different categories of human beings – some whose life must be defended and protected, some whose life can be "terminated" (that widely used euphemism for killing)?

With regard to the victims of rape, the Rev. J.G.Grant, of Troon, is reported as asking why should "the innocent victim of wickedness be condemned to bear the consequences." Won't he spare a thought for the other "innocent victim" who pays a much higher penalty by forfeiting life?

The attitude that abortion should be advocated when the unborn child is known to be handicapped is particularly worrying. It reveals a vision of the human race as some kind of exclusive club. What then, of those who become handicapped after birth – are they also to be considered for "termination"?

Extract 3

KIRK AND ABORTION

In decisively reversing last year's rigid anti-abortion line the General Assembly of the Church of Scotland, in the words of one commissioner, has returned to the ways of common sense and compassion. The more relaxed policy adopted yesterday is no daring leap forward for the Kirk but a considered return to its previous stances and a recognition that last year's departure, narrowly supported at the time, was a mistake. As one opponent of that policy argued at the time, we are dealing with the real world of brutality and suffering and not one of arid theological theories.

The policy not only put the Church in a bad light, making it appear narrow and uncaring, but evidently had a negative effect . . . by hindering the scope for pastoral ministry. As members of the chaplaincy staff in Scottish hospitals pointed out in a letter to this newspaper, many people have hesitated to consult ministers and elders while some committed Christian doctors and nurses have been placed in an impossible position.

The more moderate and realistic attitude adopted yesterday is, it has been made clear, not the assembly's final word on the subject. It still leaves scope for differences of opinion about the proper limits of abortion, a subject that medical advances have made even more complex. But there must surely be a strong consensus behind the decision taken yesterday that it is wrong to force rape victims to give birth, wrong to insist that teenagers become mothers long before they are fit for the task of motherhood, and wrong to refuse abortion when it is known that the child will be severely handicapped. This is not pandering to a secular society but returning to a position that, in the eyes of very many people both outside and within the Church, appears more firmly rooted in Christian values than the oppressive attitude that it replaces.

The Glasgow Herald 21/5/86

Without doubt, offering abortion is a soft option. It is not a response offered by a caring society. A caring society would provide a wide range of alternatives, finance medical research, and would offer such support and encouragement at both pre- and post-natal stages that no pregnant woman felt abandoned or pressurised or prey to despair. Such undertakings required dedication, total commitment, and a great deal of hard work. This is certainly not the easy option. However, should Christians expect the correct to be easy?

Referring to Scripture rather than public opinion for guidance we find Jesus constantly asking people to shoulder heavy burdens and undertake tasks which were seemingly impossible.

Isn't this where the element of faith comes in? Aren't we forgetting His message – "Take up your cross and follow Me"?

The Glasgow Herald 27/5/86

Extract 5

Kirk takes middle ground on abortion

The Church of Scotland is as divided and confused on the issue of abortion as ever although a move yesterday to return to a hard-line position was decisively defeated.

In 1985 the Assembly resolved that abortion could only be justified when the mother's life was at risk. The following year's Assembly widened this to include risk of mental or physical injury to the mother.

Early on in yesterday's proceedings there was an attempt to return to the 1985 position. The Rev. David Prentis led the move. "We are not dealing with an abstract principle, we are dealing with people whose lives are in danger," he said.

"We preach the Gospel of love to all people and that must include the tiny unborn. Jesus Christ always identified with the poor and the weak and raised the position of children as the greatest in the Kingdom of God. The weakest are the centre of the Kingdom of God and so are the disabled unborn."

He said that we are judged by our attitude to the weak which included the unborn and that there was a danger of the Church compromising its integrity on this issue.

He said that much was made out of the need to be compassionate to the mother. "It's not compassionate in a deep sense just to get her out of a fix. It is betrayal of motherhood. It's never compassionate."

The most telling contribution against the proposal came from an elderly woman in the galleries who did not identify herself: "I am probably the only woman here today who had an abortion. I was told I was going to have a child who would be a crippled imbecile. I prayed and the answer came – 'What woman in her right mind brings a child into this world who would be a burden to itself and everyone else?' So I had the abortion." She said that she now had three normal children able to serve their God.

The return to the 1985 position was then overwhelmingly rejected.

The Glasgow Herald 25/5/88

Extract 6

Vatican City: Pope John today sharply condemned euthanasia for babies born with malformations, telling doctors that no one has a "right" to a healthy child. Speaking at a European congress of pre-natal medicine, he deplored what he called the "temptation to interrupt innocent life, especially when it is not perfect and not completely healthy."

The Glasgow Herald 25/4/88

Extract 7

POPE HITS AT 'MASSACRE OF INNOCENTS'

The Pope today condemned abortion as a "massacre of innocents" and in hard-hitting remarks said states which supported it could no longer claim to defend innocent human life.

"In the past twenty years numerous states have abandoned the dignity of being defenders of innocent human life by legislating in favour of abortion.

"A real massacre of innocents is being carried out in the world every day," the Pope said.

He also criticised clerics who questioned Pope Paul VI's 1968 encyclical *Humanae Vitae*, which banned contraception.

He said the logic behind contraception was "anti-life" and its roots "a rebellion against God the Creator."

The Glasgow Herald 15/3/88

Extract 8

Dishonesty and Contraception

Sir, – Married people have insights that the clergy need to listen to and a two-way debate is needed . . . What of sex in marriage as a reconciler, as a builder of good memories so that a couple can stand tough days should they come, as a spontaneous, loving act, of the difficulties of migrant workers or seamen, of growing overpopulation in hungry lands?

The crunch issue, of course, is whether or not the authorities have got it wrong. Millions of lay people imply that they have, with immense repercussions for the nature of Church authority and how it is arrived at and how it functions. Father Walls says that throughout the world hosts of Catholics and others rejoice to follow the lead given by the Church's condemnation of contraception. That is a wildly inaccurate statement. A study of international Church documentation over many years showed over-all something like a half to three-quarters of the laity saying they did not believe contraception was wrong.

Rennie McOwan

Extract 9

PASTORAL CONCERN

Sir, – If many thousands of intelligent and well-informed Catholics are tragically and wrongly lost to their Church it should not be due to a lack of pastoral concern on the part of the Church. The Church is aware of the difficulties of life, married life included, and advises step-by-step advance to the attainment of happiness, peace and harmony.

What the Church is trying to teach is responsible parenthood. A responsible decision is usually characterised by the fact that it takes into account all the relevant factors. Parents, in deciding the number of children, are advised to take into account their duties towards themselves, their duties towards their families, all their duties towards human society, and towards God, the Creator and Author of all life. A right order of priorities will also form part of a responsible decision.

Many questions arise from this. In regard to the Creator, we so often say, "Thy will be done." But who has the authority to interpret the will of the Creator in this most important topic?

*Joseph Boyle, St Andrew's Cathedral
House
The Glasgow Herald 16/4/85*

TEST YOUR UNDERSTANDING

Extracts 1 and 2
● Why is abortion on demand rejected?
● What is the only situation when, it is argued, an abortion should be allowed?
● How should the Church help those who have an unwanted pregnancy?

Extract 3
● State in your own words the reasons put forward against the General Assembly's 1985 decision on abortion.

Extract 4
● Why, according to this extract, is it wrong to offer abortion under any circumstance?
● What particular arguments are put forward against abortion
  a) in a case of rape,
  b) where the foetus is known to be handicapped?

Extract 5
● State in your words the argument which the Rev. David Prentis puts forward against abortion?
● What is the other view expressed in this extract?

Extracts 6 and 7
● How does the Pope describe abortion?
● What is his view of countries which support abortion?
● How does he support his argument that contraception is wrong?

Extracts 8 and 9
● What arguments are put forward by Rennie McOwan in support of contraception within marriage?
● What different views are expressed in these two extracts about how decisions about what is right and wrong should be made?

PRAYERS AND THANKSGIVING FOR FORTY YEARS OF PEACE

Few flags flew in grey Westminster as the fortieth anniversary of the end of the Second World War in Europe was commemorated in Westminster Abbey yesterday.

Security was tight as members of the royal family took their seats . . . The Government was present in force, led by the Prime Minister . . . So were representatives of the Opposition and a phalanx of ambassadors – among them those of both the Federal Republic of Germany and the German Democratic Republic, the Soviet Union, Italy, and Japan. The service was split into four parts: thanksgiving: penitence: reconciliation and healing; and hope and dedication. Moving prayers of thanksgiving were spoken by the Right Rev. John Paterson, Moderator of the General Assembly of the Church of Scotland; thanksgiving "for mothers who, under strain, kept families and homes together; for acts of compassion and caring, relieving the violence of war; for the courage of those who still bear the scars of war."

In a second procession, leaders of Christian churches from across the world followed candles lit at the grave of the Unknown Warrior, through the nave, to the sanctuary where they were set around a tall Easter candle. There the Archbishop of Canterbury, Dr. Robert Runcie, greeted his fellow churchmen.

The Cardinal Archbishop of Westminster, Dr Basil Hume, led the prayers of penitence – "for not keeping faith in days of peace with those who died, and for not measuring up to the splendour of their sacrifice." A young nurse, in cape and high, frilled cap, read the lesson from the Sermon on the Mount that set the note of reconciliation and healing. In his sermon Dr Runcie made it very clear that for him war in 1939 was the lesser of two evils. "No historical inquiry," he said, "has suggested that Nazism was less wicked than we thought it in 1939, or that any other method than war could have brought it down. It was not a panacea for every ill. But the victory which closed down Belsen, Buchenwald and Auschwitz is in itself sufficient cause for thanksgiving.

"The War," he continued, "has also given us a forty-year breathing space in Europe, and the time has not been wasted. Old enemies have become friends in active co-operation."

The hope and dedication part of the service began with the third lesson, from Philippians, read by the Duke of Edinburgh. This was followed by an imaginative and symbolic act. Blazered boys and girls from the Royal Ballet School carrying small posies of white flowers processed through the nave, to meet others from the north and south transepts and move slowly into the sanctuary, where the flowers were arranged to form a cross.

The Rev. Malcolm Weisman, Senior Jewish Chaplain to the Forces, concluded the act of dedication: "We pledge ourselves to further God's perfect Kingdom by our determination to save succeeding generations from the scourge of war."

No one, as this service made clear, has any illusions as to the patience and constant watchfulness, this pledge entails.

The Glasgow Herald 9/5/85

Extract 1

Extract 2

CHURCHES ASKED TO RING BELLS FOR HIROSHIMA

Churches of all denominations in Strathclyde have been asked to ring their bells on Tuesday, August 6th, to commemorate the fortieth anniversary of the dropping of the first atomic bomb on Hiroshima. Strathclyde regional convener Councillor James Burns has written to more than five hundred clergymen asking them to ring their church bells at 8.15 a.m. on that date, the exact time that the bomb exploded in 1945 . . .

Mr Burns has asked the clergymen to include the international prayer for peace in their service on Sunday, August 4th.

Last night, however, disharmony crept into the proceedings. The Rev. Dr. Alexander Lawson, of Kilbowie Parish Church, Clydebank, said: "I don't think that we can ask the Government in the name of Jesus Christ to ignore its responsibilities to defend our people and at the moment we unfortunately need nuclear weapons and Nato to provide that defence."

At the neighbouring Abbotsford Church the bells might ring but only because the Rev. Stewart Borthwick will be away on holiday. He said: "If I was here they would not be ringing, but I'll be in Majorca. It's not that I am opposed to CND, but because I am old enough to remember when the bells were rung on VJ-DAY to signify victory over the Japanese. I think it would be hypocritical of me to ring them now when I remember how relieved everyone was at that time."

The Glasgow Herald 30/7/85

Extract 5

SLOGAN DAUBING NUNS ARRESTED

Nuns and priests were among fifty seven people arrested by police yesterday after slogans were daubed on the Ministry of Defence building in London during a military-style peace movement protest. The operation by members of the Christian Peace Movement, which was co-ordinated by clergy with walkie-talkies, coincided with the thirtieth anniversary of the Campaign for Nuclear Disarmament.

Nuns hitched up their skirts, climbed over barriers, and dodged lines of police to daub slogans such as "Repent" and "Peace" in ash that had been specially blessed for the occasion.

The Rev. Paul Bayes, chairman of Christian CND, said all sixty three people in the demonstration had intended to get arrested.

"Today is Ash Wednesday, the beginning of the period of repentance in the Church. The MOD is where nuclear wars are planned and we are asking them to repent," he said.

"The people here today are normally law-abiding, but on this issue the only way they can show the depth of their feeling is to break the law of the land."

In Glasgow, peace activists held a service of repentance outside the Ministry of Defence building. About thirty demonstrators from Christian CND and the Iona Community sang hymns and prayed for forgiveness for "The misuse of God's resources." Later they burned newspaper headlines about war and nuclear weapons, and used the ash to daub their foreheads with crosses.

The demonstrators, who included members of the clergy, were led by the Church of Scotland, who said the military expenditure of the world was more than eight thousand pounds every fifteen seconds while a child died of starvation every fifteen seconds.

"We wanted as Christians to use the beginning of Lent to express the repentance we feel at the amount of money that goes towards military spending, and to contrast it with the poverty that exists in the world," he said.

The Glasgow Herald 18/2/88

Extract 3

Heart of matter

Sir – Let us come to the heart of the matter. In churches of every denomination prayers for peace are said every Sunday without fail as part of the normal order of worship.

In every parish of the land the church bells ring out every Sunday without fail as an invitation to prayer and worship. There is no need for any dramatic special occasion. Any and every Sunday those who hear the sound of church bells are summoned to respond and pray for peace.

*Roderick McLeod, Lochwinnoch
Parish Church*

Extract 4

APARTHEID

The Roman Catholic Archbishop of Durban said yesterday the church might be forced to accept that violence was the only way to overturn apartheid.

Speaking to reporters outside St Patrick's Cathedral in New York, Archbishop Denis Hurley called for international sanctions and said: "Violence is always a very regrettable development, but there is a long history in Christian tradition of just wars and just violence. We have to accept this." He was convinced the unrest and fighting in South Africa would not end until apartheid had been defeated.

The Glasgow Herald 23/6/86

TEST YOUR UNDERSTANDING

Extract 1
- List the four parts into which the service was divided and write a brief note about each part.
- What evidence is there, from the list of people attending the service, that 'reconciliation and healing' has taken place?
- How does Dr Runcie support Britain's decision to go to war in 1939?
- State in your own words the pledge made by the senior Jewish chaplain to the forces.

Extract 2
- Why were churches in Strathclyde asked to ring their bells?
- What reasons are given for not agreeing to this request?

Extract 3
- What additional reason is given in this extract for not agreeing to the request to ring church bells?

Extract 4
- What do you think is meant by the phrases 'just war' and 'just violence'?

Extract 5
- Why did the Christian Peace Movement carry out their protest on Ash Wednesday?
- Why did the demonstrators from Christian CND and the Iona Community ask for forgiveness?

Database

A database on contemporary Christianity called News Line *has been developed at Jordanhill College of Education, Glasgow, in order to keep up with this changing new world. Each day* The Glasgow Herald, *one of Scotland's main newspapers, is examined for articles and reports on what Christians are saying and doing over a wide range of issues, including some of the ones in this chapter.*

Some of these issues concern beliefs and practices relating to Christianity itself, e.g. Easter, Worship. Most of them, however, are about concerns which affect all people whether they hold any religious beliefs or not, e.g. War, Peace, Sexual Relationships.

News Line *comes in two-year packages. The first package covers 1985-6 and includes references to over 50 different Christian churches or organisations and 70 issues. The discs are for use with a BBC Micro computer. Full particulars are available from Sales and Publications, Jordanhill College of Education, 76 Southbrae Drive, Glasgow G13 1PP (Tel. 041-950 3170/71).*

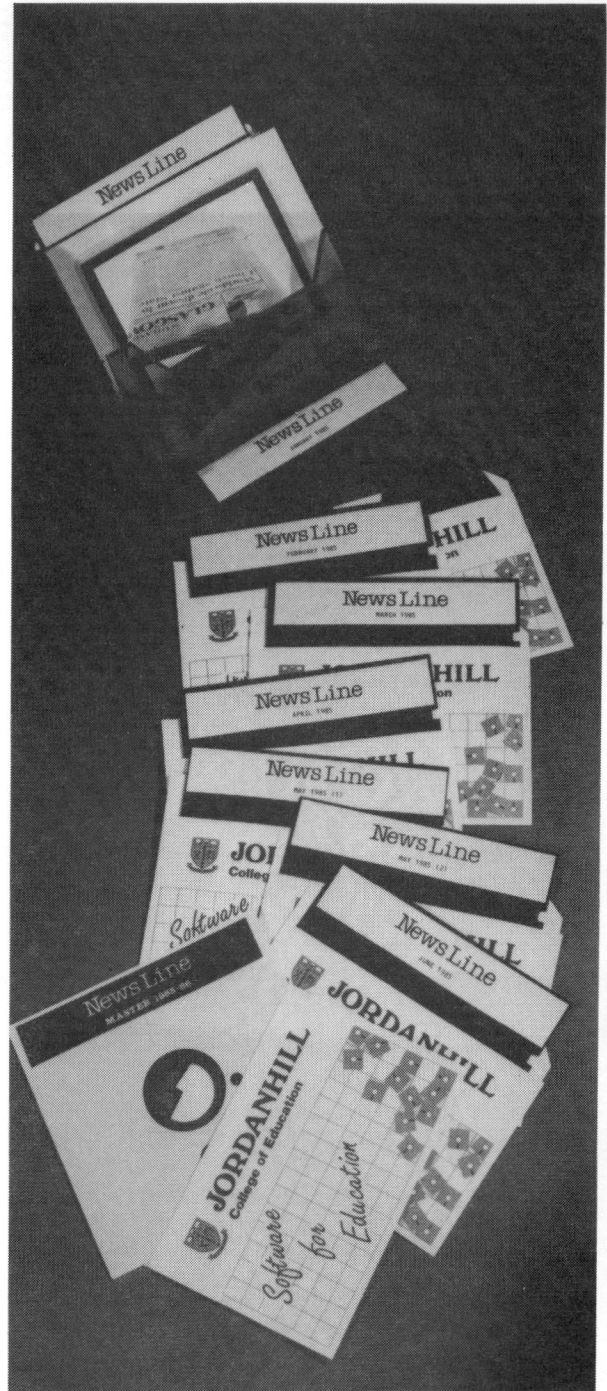

SEARCH: THE CHRISTIAN EXPERIENCE

What can we learn about our search into how Christians answer our four questions?

> Where do we come from?
> What are we?
> Where are we going?
> How do we get there?

Where Do We Come From?

Like many of the questions which have teased and puzzled men and women through the centuries, this question can be explored at different levels.
We could say:
'We come from our parents' or,
'We come from our home town, or the United Kingdom, or Europe' or,
'We come from the 20th century'.
In our modern world of space travel, Star Trek and E.T. we could even say:
'We come from the planet Earth'.
Each of these answers tells us something about ourselves.
When the artist Gauguin asked the question, he was probing for a deeper and more important answer. At this level, the Christian answer is:
'We come from God'. Or to use the traditional language of the Nicene Creed, God is:
'Maker of heaven and earth, and of all things visible and invisible.'
What this means, so far as men and women are concerned, is worked out more fully for Christians in their answer to our second question.

What Are We?

Following the Christian answer to the previous question we can say: 'We are part of God's creation'. Television news programmes and newspaper reports, however, remind us that though there is much evidence of courage and selfless action in the world today, there is also a darker side to life. As the articles on Easter Today indicate this 'darkness' may show itself at times in acts of violence inflicted by one individual on another, at other times in acts of terrorism or warfare. In the light of all of this, what have Christians to say about people's relationship to God, their creator?
Our best answer here is in the opening words of the Lord's prayer:
'Our Father who art in heaven'.
Christians believe that men and women are 'children of God', though as the parable of the Prodigal Son suggests, they often act as disobedient children who like to go their own way.

117

But the emphasis in Jesus' teaching is not on people and their behaviour. It is on the love and forgiveness of God the Father. We shall see this again in our exploration of the fourth and final question.

Where Are We Going?

Jesus was not concerned only with pictures of what people are like. He was also concerned with what people could be. His teaching on loving enemies and his parable of the Good Samaritan spell out what people could and should be like. These qualities are summed up in the prayer of St Francis:

'Lord, make me an instrument of your peace.
Where there is hatred, let me bring love;
Where there is injury, pardon;
Where there is doubt, faith;
Where there is despair, hope;
Where there is darkness, light;
Where there is sadness, let me bring joy'.

Few could claim to have measured up to this ideal. As the articles on Christmas and Easter Today show, however, Christians are called to share these qualities and live more fully as 'sons of God' or as 'members of God's Kingdom'.

The question 'Where are we going?' could also be answered at a different level. Christians believe that life is not ended at the grave. The words and rituals of the Christian funeral service point to Jesus as the key to real life, and to the belief that this life is not extinguished by death.

'I am the resurrection and the life;
He who believes in me, even if he is dead, shall live;
and all who live and believe in me, will never die.'

How Do We Get There?

We have seen in our exploration of the second question that the love and forgiveness of God is central to the teaching of Jesus. This, in fact, is the key to the Christian answer to our fourth and final question. Christians believe that it is God who takes the lead in helping people to grow from what they are to what they could be. The central acts by which God does this are celebrated in the great festivals of the Christian calendar. In weekly worship with other Christians and at the personal milestones of life, Christians receive God's help in reaching their goal.

But Christians believe that people themselves have also their part to play. The Church has always stressed the duty of Church members to make regular use of the sacraments and the good news of the Bible.

The true sign of people's growth can be seen both in their worship of God and in their service to others. Jesus expressed this idea in his introduction to the parable of the Good Samaritan:

'Love the Lord your God with all your heart,
with all your soul,
with all your strength,
and with all your mind'
and
'Love your neighbour as you love yourself.'

The Search: The End or the Beginning?

As we have seen in our search of the Christian experience, Christians do not always agree on how best to 'love God and love your neighbour'.

In the past, many Christians believed that their way of worship and their solutions to the big issues of life were the only correct ones. Today there is a greater willingness to try out new ways of worship and to consider new ways of tackling the challenges of the 20th century. The basic beliefs remain but the search always continues for new ways of testing them in our ever changing world.

WORD LIST

Absolution   Literally, 'set free'. The forgiveness of sins declared by a priest to those who confess and are sorry for their wrong-doing.

Adoration   The act of reverent worship which is due to God alone.

Advent   Literally, 'the coming'. The Christian season which includes the four Sundays leading to Christmas. Advent begins the Calendar of the Christian Year.

Agnus Dei   The Latin words for 'Lamb of God', a title of Christ used in the Eucharist or Holy Communion.

Aisle   Literally, 'a wing'. A passage, usually at the side of a church, which separates one row of seats from another.

Alb   Literally, 'white'. A long white tunic worn by a priest at Mass.

Allegory   A form of story full of symbolic meanings.

Alleluia   (Sometimes spelt 'Hallelujah'). A shout of praise to God, from two Hebrew words meaning 'Praise Jah'. It is found at the beginning or end of some of the Psalms.

Alms   A gift, usually of money, given for the poor.

Altar   A raised table in the sanctuary of a church used for the Mass or Eucharist.

Amen   A Hebrew word meaning 'truly' or 'so let it be,' which is said or sung by the worshippers at the end of prayers and hymns.

Amice   A piece of linen cloth covering the shoulder of a priest at Mass.

Angel   A messenger from God, often pictured in art as a winged figure.

Anglican   Belonging to the Church of England and churches which have similar beliefs, organization, and forms of worship.

Anoint   To apply oil or ointment. Anointing is a very ancient religious sign of God's favour. In Old Testament times priests and kings were anointed. Nowadays Christian anointing may be done in some Churches at Baptism, Confirmation, and for the sick and dying.

Anthem   A song of praise with words from Scripture usually sung by a choir in church.

Antidoron   A small piece of bread which is blessed and given to the worshippers at the close of the service in an Orthodox Church.

Apostles   Literally, 'sent'. The name given in the New Testament to the twelve disciples chosen by Jesus and sent to preach the Gospel. The name is also applied to Paul and Barnabas who were early Christian missionaries.

Apostles' Creed   An ancient short summary of Christian belief which was recited at baptism services in the early Church. It goes back to the 2nd century but is named after the apostles to give it authority and respect. The Apostles' Creed is regularly repeated in most branches of the Christian Church as a basic statement of faith.

Apostolic   In agreement with the teaching of the New Testament apostles. Their lifetime is known as the Apostolic Age.

Aramaic   The common language of Palestine spoken by the Jews in the time of Jesus. There are some Aramaic words and phrases here and there in the Gospels, e.g. 'Talitha koum' in Mark 5: 41.

Archbishop   The chief bishop with authority over a number of bishops and with spiritual government of an area of the Church.

Ascension   The ascent of Jesus to heaven after his resurrection (Luke 24: 50-53). The day is celebrated on the Thursday forty days after Easter.

Baptism   Literally, 'dip'. A Christian sacrament using water as a sign of the admission of a person to the Christian Church.

Baptist   A branch of the Christian Church in which the sacrament of baptism is administered to adult believers only, by total immersion in water.

Bead   Literally, 'prayer'. A small ball or bead strung on a rosary for counting off prayers as they are recited. Hence the saying: 'telling one's beads'.

Beatitude   Beatitude means a special blessing or happiness. Throughout the Bible we find such phrases as 'Blessed is the man who . . .' The name is specially applied to the sayings of Jesus at the beginning of his teaching (see Luke 6: 20–23), e.g.
  'Happy are you poor;
  The Kingdom of God is yours!'

Benediction   A short blessing in the name of God, usually given by the priest or minister at the end of public worship.

Benedictus   The Latin name for the Song of Zechariah in Luke 1: 67-80.

Bishop   Literally, 'overseer'. A clergyman who rules over a district of the Church and over the priests and deacons in it.

Blasphemy   Speaking abusive language about God, often in cursing or swearing.

Blessed Sacrament   A name for the Eucharist, applied especially to the bread and wine.

Blessing   The declaration of God's favour. Often used as another name for the Benediction.

Book of Common Order   The Service Book authorized by the General Assembly for use as a guide to worship in the Church of Scotland.

Candle   A wax light traditionally used on the altar or carried in procession or lit as a personal offering of devotion in church. The flickering light is a symbol of prayer and of Christ's victory over darkness and evil.

Cardinal   A high official of the Roman Catholic Church who ranks next to the Pope. The cardinals form a Council to advise the Pope, and they elect a new Pope from among their number.

120

Carol   Originally a carol was a ring dance and the happy song that went with it. Nowadays the name is mainly used of Christmas songs or hymns.

Cassock   A long loose outer robe worn by clergy and, in some churches, by members of the choir.

Catechism   A book of questions and answers used to teach a new member of the Church the basic facts and beliefs of the Christian faith.

Cathedral   The leading church in a diocese or bishop's district. One of its furnishings is the bishop's throne.

Catholic   Literally, 'universal'. It means the whole body of Christians, as in the Creed: *'I believe in the holy catholic Church'* ... that is, those who claim to be part of the ancient, worldwide Christian Church.

Censer   A metal dish in which incense is burned. It is usually swung on chains during a church service.

Chalice   A cup or bowl used for the wine in the sacrament of the Mass or Holy Communion.

Chaplain   A minister or priest appointed to a hospital, school, prison, industrial works, or the armed forces.

Charismatic   An extraordinary power given to a Christian for the good of the Church. The Charismatic Movement of recent times reminds Christians of the early days of the Church when every member received gifts of the Spirit to teach, to heal, to speak in tongues.

Chasuble   The outermost vestment worn by a priest when celebrating Mass.

Choir   This word means the group who lead the singing in a church. It is also the name given to the part of the church which they occupy.

Christ   The Greek name which is the equivalent of the Hebrew 'Messiah' and means 'the anointed'. It is the title given by believers to Jesus of Nazareth and the name from which 'Christian' comes.

Christendom   The part of the world where Christianity is the main religion. A collective word for all Christians.

Christian   A believer in and follower of Jesus Christ. A member of one of the Christian Churches. It was originally a nickname given to Jesus' followers in Antioch. See Acts 11: 26.

Christian Calendar   The order of the main dates of the Christian Year which runs from Advent and includes such festivals as Christmas, Easter, Whitsun.

Christmas   The annual festival held on 25th December when the birth of Jesus is commemorated.

Church   The whole body of Christian believers. The word is also used of individual denominations of Christians and of the buildings they worship in.

Cincture   A woven cord or band worn round the waist by the clergy when they are robed for a Church service. Also known as a girdle.

Circumcision   The cutting of the foreskin of an infant boy. Circumcision is observed by the Jews as a sign that the boy is part of the Jewish community.

Clergy   The ordained ministers or priests of the Christian Church.

Collect   A short prayer of one main sentence, containing one petition or request.

Communion   Literally, 'common'. The Christian sacrament in which bread and wine are used to commemorate the death of Christ.

Confession   Acknowledgment of sin or fault in the form of a prayer to God, made either privately or to a priest as God's representative.

Confirmation   The rite by which one is admitted to full communion in most branches of the Church. Candidates renew the vows taken at their Baptism and the bishop or minister prays that they may receive the Holy Spirit.

Congregation   A group of people belonging to and attending a particular church. A body of people assembled for worship.

Congregationalist   A member of a Protestant Church which is strongly independent and stresses the importance of the local congregation.

Consecrated/Consecration   Set apart by a religious prayer or rite. The part of the service of the Eucharist or Holy Communion in which the bread and wine are made sacred.

Council   A formal assembly of bishops or other Church leaders who decide doctrine or discipline.

Counter-Reformation   The reform movement within the Roman Catholic Church following the Protestant Reformation of the 16th century.

Covenant   Literally, 'coming together'. A solemn agreement between God and a person or people in which both sides make their promise. The idea of a covenant between God and his chosen people runs all through the Bible. The word 'Testament' has the same meaning, and gives its name to the two main divisions of the Bible.

Creed   Literally, 'I believe'. A statement which summarizes religious beliefs, as in the Apostles' Creed and the Nicene Creed.

Cross   The symbol of the Christian faith, recalling the wooden cross on which Jesus was crucified.

Deacon   A member of the order of clergy ranking below a priest in the Roman Catholic, Orthodox, and Anglican Churches.

Dedicated   Set apart for the worship of God or for some sacred purpose.

Denomination   A body of Christians sharing the same name and with the same beliefs.

Disciple   Literally, 'a learner'. One who follows and learns from another. Used especially of the twelve men Jesus invited to follow him.

Doctrine   A statement of the beliefs of a Christian Church.

Dogma   Teaching about faith or morals stated with the full authority of the Church.

Dove   The bird which is a Biblical and Christian symbol of innocence, gentleness, peace, and the Holy Spirit of God.

Doxology   Literally, 'speaking glory'. A short act of praise to God, said or sung. It usually names 'the Father, the Son, and the Holy Spirit'.

Easter The festival which commemorates the resurrection of Christ, the greatest and the oldest feast of the Christian Church.

Ecumenical Belonging to the universal, world-wide Christian Church. The word is used of world-wide Christian unity and co-operation between Churches.

Elder An ordained office-bearer in the Presbyterian Church who serves on the kirk session and assists the minister in Holy Communion. The name is a translation of the New Testament word 'presbyter'.

Elevation The lifting up of the bread and wine of the Eucharist so that they may be seen by all the people.

Epistle A letter or writing sent to an individual or a Church, e.g. the Epistles of Paul in the New Testament. A lesson from the Epistles is read in most Christian Churches at Sunday morning service.

Eucharist Literally, 'thanksgiving'. The Christian sacrament which commemorates the death of Christ and gives thanks for its meaning. The central act of Christian worship, otherwise known as the Mass or Holy Communion.

Evangelism The preaching of the Gospel from place to place, and the winning of people to a personal faith in Christ.

Faith Trust or belief, usually used of trust in a loving God. 'The Christian Faith' means the beliefs based on the Bible, the Creeds, and the teaching of the Church.

Fasting To go without food as a religious duty. Fasting used to be a common religious custom and it is still observed by some believers on certain days of the Christian Year.

Festival A time of joy to commemorate some great religious event, e.g. Christmas, Easter, often kept as a holiday.

Font Literally, 'a fountain'. A container for holding the water for the sacrament of baptism.

Fraction The breaking of the bread in the Eucharist or Holy Communion.

Frankincense A fragrant gum used in incense. The gift of frankincense brought by the visitors from the East to the infant Jesus was a symbol of worship.

General Assembly The highest Court of the Church of Scotland.

Gentile Anyone who is not a Jew.

Gloria The Latin first word of the phrase: *'Glory be to God on high'* or *'Glory be to the Father'*.

Gospel Literally, 'good story' or 'good news'. The four books of the New Testament by Matthew, Mark, Luke and John, which tell the story of the life and work, death and resurrection of Jesus.

Gown A loose, flowing outer garment worn by the clergy.

Grace A short prayer at the end of the service or before a meal, giving thanks to God.

Greek Biblical Greek was the language in which the New Testament was written. It was the common tongue of the Mediterranean world of that time.

Hail Mary A Roman Catholic prayer to the Virgin Mary asking for her help.

Heathen One who is outside organized religion or who is ignorant of it.

Hebrew The ancient name for the ancestors of the Jewish people and for their language. Most of the Old Testament was written in Hebrew.

Heresy An opinion or belief which is against Church teaching.

Holy Perfect and pure in a sacred way. A term particularly applied to God in prayer, or used about things set apart for the service of God, e.g. Holy Table.

Holy Family The baby Jesus with his mother Mary and Joseph.

Holy Ghost Another name for the Holy Spirit.

Holy Spirit The third person of the Christian Trinity. The active presence of God in people's lives.

Holy Table A name for the altar or communion table in church, from which the bread and wine of the Eucharist are served to worshippers.

Holy Week The week before Easter, during which the main events of the last days of Jesus' life are commemorated.

Homily A plain, practical sermon spoken to the congregation.

Hospice A Christian hospital or home maintained by a Church for people who are incurably ill.

Hymn A song of praise, usually applied to Christian worship.

Icon Literally, 'likeness' or 'image'. A picture, usually painted on wood, to show Jesus or one of the saints, and used as an object of devotion in the Orthodox Church.

Icon Screen A screen covered with icons in an Orthodox church which shuts off the sanctuary.

Incarnation The Christian term for the birth of Jesus, literally meaning 'in the flesh'.

Incense Spices and gums which are burned in religious rites to give a sweet-smelling smoke, a symbol of prayer.

Intercession Prayer on behalf of others.

Jew A member of the Jewish race or religion, descended from the Hebrew people whose story is told in the Old Testament.

Kirk Session The lowest Court of the Church of Scotland, consisting of the minister and the elders of the congregation.

Kyrie Eleison Two Greek words which literally mean 'Lord, have mercy'. This short prayer is said in the Mass and in the Communion Service of all the main branches of the Church.

Laity Ordinary members of the Church who do not belong to the clergy.

Last Supper   The meal which Jesus shared with his disciples on the night he was betrayed. It is the origin of the Eucharist or Holy Communion, the central sacrament of the Church.

Lectern   A church reading-desk from which the Bible is read. It is often in the form of a wooden or brass eagle with outstretched wings.

Legend   A wonderful story about a famous person or event. Often a story handed down about a saint.

Lent   The forty days from Ash Wednesday to Easter. Lent is kept by Christians as a time of penitence and prayer.

Litany   An ancient form of prayer which began in the Eastern Church, made up of a series of petitions with responses by the congregation.

Liturgy   The regular rites or pattern of worship of a church.

Magnificat   The Latin name for the Song of Mary, from Luke 1: 46-55.

Mass   The name for the celebration of the Eucharist in the Roman Catholic Church.

Messiah   The Hebrew word for 'the anointed'. The title was given to the expected son of David who would deliver the Jewish people from their sufferings and bring about God's Kingdom. The name 'Christ' is the Greek form of the same word.

Methodist   The Methodist Church began with the preaching of John Wesley in the 18th century.

Minister   Literally, 'a servant'. The ordained clergyman in charge of a Reformed Church, e.g. the Church of Scotland. His special duties are to preach and to administer the sacraments.

Missal   The book which contains the words and devotions for the service of the Mass throughout the year in the Roman Catholic Church.

Missionary   One who is sent out to preach the Gospel, usually in a foreign land.

Moderator   The minister who is chairman of a Court of the Church of Scotland, e.g. of the Kirk Session, General Assembly.

Myrrh   A bitter fragrant gum from an Eastern tree. Myrrh was one of the gifts brought by the visitors from the East to the infant Jesus. Myrrh is traditionally the symbol of suffering and death.

Nave   The main part of the inside of a church building, where the worshippers sit.

Nicene Creed   The Creed of the Church which goes back to the Council of Nicea in A.D. 325. It is still recited in the main branches of the Church as the central statement of their faith.

Nunc Dimittis   The Latin name for the Song of Simeon in Luke 2: 29 - 32.

Ordained   Appointed or set apart officially by religious authority to a position in the ministry of the Church, e.g. ordained as a priest or as a minister.

Orders   Various ranks in the ministry of the Church, e.g. bishop, priest, deacon.

Palm Sunday   The Sunday before Easter. It is associated with a procession which reminds worshippers of the triumphal entry of Jesus into Jerusalem.

Parable   A parable is a comparison, literally, 'placed side by side', for example, *'the Kingdom of heaven is like a mustard seed'*. The parables of Jesus are true-to-life stories which invite us to learn some truth.

Parish   A district in the community with its own church and minister or priest.

Pasch/Paschal   An old name for the Jewish festival of Passover and the Christian festival of Easter, and also for the customs associated with Easter, e.g. Paschal candle: a large candle blessed and placed on the altar in the Roman Catholic Church.

Passion   The sufferings and death of Christ, especially the crucifixion.

Passover   The most important festival of the Jewish religious year. It commemorates the events that led up to the Exodus from Egypt under Moses. In New Testament times the Passover was celebrated in Jerusalem. Nowadays it is kept in the Jewish home

Paten   The plate, usually of silver or gold, to hold the bread at the Eucharist or Holy Communion.

Patriarch   The head of an area of the Orthodox Church, e.g. Patriarch of Constantinople.

Penitence   Showing sorrow for sin or wrong-doing.

Petition   The simplest form of prayer, asking for a blessing or for help, e.g. *'Give us this day our daily bread.'*

Pew   A fixed wooden bench in a church.

Pharisees   The name means 'separated'. The Pharisees were a Jewish group in New Testament times who were known and respected for their strict keeping of the written and unwritten Law.

Pilgrim   One who travels a long way to visit a holy place.

Pope   The bishop of Rome and head of the Roman Catholic Church. The name literally means 'father'.

Presbyter   The Greek word means 'elder' or 'overseer'. The name is given to an elder or minister of a Presbyterian Church, such as The Church of Scotland.

Presbyterian   A form of Church government in which the Church is ruled by presbyters or elders in a series of self-governing Courts, e.g. Kirk Session, General Assembly.

Priest   The name given to a clergyman in many branches of the Church. Especially a Roman Catholic clergyman in charge of a local church whose special task is the celebration of the Mass.

Protestant   Literally, 'one who protests'. The name was first given to Christians who denied the authority of the Pope at the time of the Reformation. A Protestant claims the Bible as his only authority.

Psalms   The devotional poems and songs in the Old Testament Book of Psalms which are now continually used in public worship of the Christian Church.

Pulpit   A raised desk or closed-in box in a church for preaching.

Rabbi   A Hebrew word meaning 'master' or 'teacher'. The rabbis in New Testament times taught the words and meaning of the Jewish Law.

Reconciliation   Friendship or peace restored between two people or parties.

Reformation   The religious movement in the 16th century which led to the rejection of the authority of the Pope and the rule of the Roman Catholic Church.

Reformed   A branch of the Church based on the principles of the Reformation.

Resurrection   The rising of Christ from the dead which is a central part of Christian teaching.

Ritual   The regular ordered way of performing worship or a rite of the Church.

Rosary   A string of beads which Roman Catholic and Orthodox worshippers use when reciting prayers of devotion.

Sabbath   The sacred day of the Jewish week (Saturday) when all normal work is forbidden. The Sabbath is set apart for the worship of God and as a day of rest and joy.

Sacrament   The most famous description of a sacrament is: 'an outward and visible sign of an inward and spiritual grace'. It is a religious rite through which the Christian believes that he receives God's help in his day-to-day life.

Sacred   Set apart or dedicated to God.

Sadducees   A party of the Jews in New Testament times, largely made up of priests of the Temple. They held the Law of Moses to be sacred, but they did not go beyond the written letter of the Law. They were opposed to the Pharisees.

Salutation   Words of greeting, as in the Eucharist phrase: 'The Lord be with you.'

Salvation   A gift of God which sets men free from the power of sin and brings them to full health. Jesus is called the Saviour because Christians believe he brings about salvation.

Sanctuary   The most sacred part of a religious building. The name usually refers to the part where the altar or holy table stands.

Sanctus   The Latin name for the spoken prayer: 'Holy, holy, holy' used in the Eucharist or Holy Communion.

Sanhedrin   The chief religious Council of the Jews in the time of Jesus. It met in the Temple area to administer the Law and deal with those who broke it.

Satan   The name of the chief of the evil spirits, sometimes called the Devil.

Scriptures   The sacred writing of the Jewish and Christian faiths contained in the Old and New Testaments of the Bible.

Sermon   A talk from the pulpit to explain the meaning of a text from the Bible. It is usually part of the regular Church service of worship.

Sponsor   One who presents a child or a candidate for baptism and promises to be responsible for his Christian education and upbringing. A godfather or godmother.

Stole   A vestment in the form of a long narrow strip of silk worn round the neck by a priest or minister. It symbolizes the yoke of Christ.

Supplication   A prayer asking God's continuing help.

Surplice   A loose white vestment with wide sleeves worn over the cassock by the clergy during a service of worship.

Sursum Corda   The Latin name for the phrase: 'Lift up your hearts' used in the Eucharist or Holy Communion.

Symbol   A sign which stands for something else, e.g. bread and wine stand for the body and blood of Christ in the Eucharist. A visible sign of some invisible meaning.

Synagogue   The name literally means 'meeting'. The synagogue building is where Jews meet for worship.

Tabernacle   The box beside the altar in the Roman Catholic Church which contains consecrated bread and wine from the Eucharist.

Testament   See **Covenant.**

Torah   The Law of Moses contained in the first five books of the Bible: Genesis, Exodus, Leviticus, Numbers, Deuteronomy.

Tradition   The handing down of beliefs and customs by word and example from one generation to another of worshippers.

Trisagion   An ancient hymn of the Christian Church with the words: 'Holy God, holy and mighty, holy and immortal, have mercy upon us'.

Vatican   The headquarters and home of the Pope in Rome.

Vatican Council   From time to time the Roman Catholic Church has summoned Councils to state clearly what the Church believes. In modern times a very important meeting has been the Second Vatican Council, or Vatican II as it is popularly known, which met in Rome from 1962 to 1965. The main concern of Vatican II was to renew the life of the Church and to bring its teaching, worship and organization up to date and relevant to the world today.

Vestments   Clothes worn in religious ceremonies.

Vicar of Christ   A title of the Pope.

Vigil   A service of prayer held during the night, especially before Easter.

Whitsun   The Feast of the coming of the Holy Spirit which falls on the seventh Sunday after Easter.

Worship   The praise and reverence given to God.

THEMATIC INDEX

GENERAL INDEX

SOURCES AND ACKNOWLEDGMENTS

Extracts

The Glasgow Herald for the Church Notices of 8 May 1982 on page 7; and for the extracts on pages 73, 74, 83, 84, 108, 109, 110, 111, 113 and 114.

Ward Lock Educational Co. Ltd for the extract on page 79 from *The Orthodox Church* by Sergei Hackel.

The Church of Scotland for the top two extracts on page 104 and top and bottom extracts on page 105, all from *The General Assembly* 1981, 1982, 1983; bottom extract on page 104 and middle extract on page 105 from the newspaper of the Church of Scotland Board of World Mission and Unity, formerly known as *Worldscope*.

George Outram & Co. Ltd for extracts on page 100, both from the former *Sunday Standard*.

Scottish Catholic Observer for extracts on pages 99, 102 and 103.

Flourish for extracts on page 101.

Save the Children Fund for the extract from *The World's Children* on page 103 (top left).

Christian Aid for material on pages 106-7 adapted from their leaflet on El Salvador.

Photographs

Museum of Fine Arts, Boston for *'D'ou venons nous . . . Que sommes nous . . . Ou allons nous?'* by Paul Gauguin, 1897, oil on canvas, 139 x 374.5 cm, 36.270, Arthur Gordon Tompkins Fund 1936, cover; 'The Temptation and Fall of Eve' by William Blake (illustration to Paradise Lost), pen and watercolour, 50 x 38cm, 90.99, Subscription of 1890, page 39.

Dept of Medical Illustration, Royal Hospital for Sick Children, Glasgow, page 2 (top left)

Everett Pinto & Co. Ltd for A.D.A.G.P. for 'Le Surhomme pour l'Apocalypse' by P.Y. Trémois, 1961, © A.D.A.G.P. Paris 1984, page 2 (top right)

NASA, page 2 (bottom)

Philip Emmett, page 4 (top); page 19

Camera Press, page 4 (bottom), photograph by Boulahya

F.W. Feetenby and *The Universe*, page 5 (top)

Express Newspapers, page 5 (middle)

Lawrence Harnor and the *Scottish Catholic Observer*, page 5 (bottom); page 99

World Council of Churches, page 8 (symbol); page 12; page 86, photograph by J Taylor; page 91

Lothian Studios and the *Scottish Catholic Observer*, page 8

Mansell Collection, page 10

The Glasgow Herald, page 13 (left); page 78

Popperfoto, page 13 (bottom right)

George Outram & Co Ltd, page 14, photograph by Ian Hossack; page 136 (bottom)

Church of Scotland, page 17 (top left and bottom right); page 23; page 24 (bottom); page 57; page 89; page 100; page 105

David J. McCormick, page 17 (top right and bottom left); page 21; page 22

Rev K. McIlhagga, The Free Church Centre, St Ives, page 18

Rev J Simpson and Simpson Photographers, Greenock, page 24 (top)

Sotheby & Co, page 34

The Universe, page 35

Ronald Sheridan's Photo Library page 41

S.P.A.D.E.M. copyright DACS 1984, page 42

Topham, page 44

Christian Aid, page 45; shortened version of El Salvador leaflet, pages 106-7

National Catholic News Services, Washington D.C. and *Scottish Catholic Observer,* page 47, page 49

U.I.P. (U.K.) and National Film Archive, page 51

Bill Sinclair and *Scottish Catholic Observer*, page 53; page 77

Frank Spooner Pictures for Gamma, page 61, photograph by Marc Bulka

U.S.P.G. page 64

Cambridge Evening News, page 66

131

The Iona Community, page 76

Carberry Tower, Church of Scotland Residential Training and Conference Centre, Musselburgh, page 80

Scottish Television and Church of Scotland Lodging House Mission Committee, page 81

British Council of Churches, page 85, cartoon by Karen Escott

Flourish, page 88 (left), page 101

Stewart Ferguson and *Scottish Catholic Oberserver,* page 88 (right), photograph by Ethel Ferguson

James Morrison Photography and Mr and Mrs Cameron, page 93

Archives Departmentales de l'Essone (clichés pré inventaire des richesses artistiques de l'Essonne), page 95

Rev J. Canning, Greenock, page 96

Federation of British Cremation Authorities, page 98

Bel Press photographers and *Scottish Catholic Observer* page 102 (top)

Hugh Gibson, Strathclyde Studios and *Scottish Catholi Observer,* page 102 (bottom)

Save the Children Fund, page 103

Jordanhill College of Education, Glasgow, page 116